D1583600

Lanchester Library
WITHDRAWN

THE WORLD BACKWARDS
Russian futurist books 1912–16

THE WORLD BACKWARDS
Russian futurist books 1912–16

Susan P. Compton

The British Library

© 1978 The British Library Board
ISBN O 7141 0396 9 paper
     O 7141 0397 7 cased

Published by
British Museum Publications Ltd
6 Bedford Square, London WC1B 3RA

Designed by Gerald Cinamon

Typeset in Monophoto Photina
and printed in Great Britain by
Balding and Mansell Ltd
Wisbech and London

 British Library Cataloguing in Publication Data

Compton, Susan P
    The world backwards.
    1. Futurism (Art) – Russia
    I. Title
    700'.947   NX556.A1

Lanchester Polytechnic
Art and Design Library

Author   COMPTON

Class   709.71651 COM

TO MICHAEL,
JO AND TOM
AND ANN

PREFACE

A few years ago I came across a fascinating study of Russian futurism. It was like an atlas, mapping unknown territory: gripping and frustrating – boundaries were there, contours, yet there seemed to be no means of exploring the place for oneself. The book was *Russian Futurism: a history* written by Vladimir Markov just ten years ago. For anyone interested in the development of Russian art, it seemed like the directions to a hidden treasure – the contemporary record of the work of artists and writers, working together at one of the most exciting periods of the twentieth century, to invent a truly Russian, modern style.

Markov had charted the writings, but the illustrations and graphic design were what I wanted to see. The next few years were like a treasure hunt: on the look-out for clues to the whereabouts of these amazing illustrated Russian futurist publications. I found one in a library here, another there, more in America, and then M. Alexandre Polonski in Paris showed me, for the first time, a collection of the books and allowed me to photograph from them.

The publication of Professor Markov's book resulted in several important sales at Sotheby's; a remarkable collection, assembled from some of these sales, has fortunately found a permanent home at the British Library Reference Division. I would like to thank the Director General for inviting me to write this book and I hope I have been able to convey some of the enthusiasm I feel for the work of the most important writers and artists so thoroughly represented by these particular books.

I have tried to introduce several subjects which have not been studied before: the graphic design, the way the illustrations illuminate the development of avant-garde art as well as the writing; and, in one area, that of theatre, I have placed some of the material in a wider context. For the general reader the chapter providing a chronological structure will prove the hardest, yet the experiments in writing and art took place in a movement of great complexity, and I have tried to set it out so that the cooperation of poets and painters which resulted in these outstanding publications can be appreciated.

The selection of illustrations has proved a challenge: from the wealth of material in the British Library collection I have tried to show the variety of styles of illustration and graphic design. In this respect, I am most grateful to Graham Marsh of the British Library Photographic Service for the great trouble he has taken to make photographs which show the books as they are.

I would like to thank Patrick Fairs and Michael McLaren-Turner of the Slavonic Branch of the British Library for their patience and enthusiasm. Christine Thomas (of the same branch) has helped me enormously and has made an invaluable contribution by making translations for me: unless otherwise acknowledged, I have used her translation. Furthermore, Christine Thomas has checked all the dates of the books in the official contemporary publication, *Knizhnaya letopis*, in which, week by week, the details of every book passed by the censor and put on sale were registered. The information she has gathered, together with the Cyrillic title, is included in list form at the end of the book for easy reference. Russian dates are given in Old Style (according to the calendar in use in Russia before 1917) so each is thirteen days behind the rest of Europe. I have used the British system of transliteration with some modifications, notably that final 'ii' is represented by 'y' in the case of proper names. Another exception is that of artists and writers whose names are well known in the West in another form (for instance, after David Burliuk settled in the United States, Burlyuk was habitually spelt with an 'i' instead of 'y'). I have omitted the soft sign which should be represented by an apostrophe so that the name Kul'bin, for example, is thus referred to throughout as Kulbin. In order not to interrupt the narrative unduly, I have written the titles of books, exhibitions etc, in English translation (usually the one adopted by Vladimir Markov) and given the transliterated Russian only the first time a book title is mentioned in each chapter.

Finally, I would like to thank all who have given me encouragement and support in this challenging field of study: Christopher Green for suggesting I begin; Peter Vergo for great help and encouragement; Andrei Nakov for allowing me unlimited access to his archives and for sharing ideas with me; Mary Chamot, for much information and patience; Evgeny Kovtun for his scholarship from which I have gained so much; Felicity Ashbee for unfailing friendship; John Golding for painstaking criticism, so generously given. It has been a great pleasure to work with Gerald Cinamon whose skill I much appreciate.

In common with other students of this period, I owe an enormous debt to the work of Nikolai Khardzhiev, whose interesting articles have provided an important factual basis for this study. For those who wish to study the subject further in English, Professor John Bowlt has provided invaluable translations. I am most grateful to him for allowing me to use liberal quotations from *Russian Art of the Avant-Garde: Theory and Criticism 1902–34*, and from his translation of the memoirs of Benedikt Livshits, *The One and a Half-Eyed Archer*.

THE WORLD BACKWARDS
Russian futurist books 1912–16

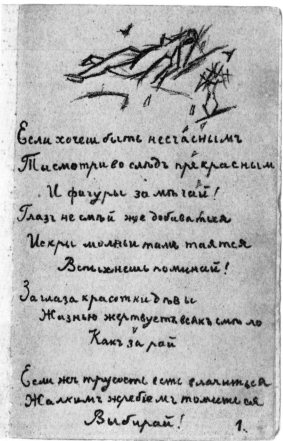

1. *Old-time Love*, 1912:
seven handwritten poems
by A. Kruchenykh.
Cover design by M. Larionov.
14.5 x 9.7 cm.

2. *Old-time Love*, 1912: p. 1,
poem by A. Kruchenykh,
'decoration' by M. Larionov.

I

INTRODUCTION

This study is mainly concerned with Russian futurist books published between 1912 and 1916 in Moscow and St Petersburg. In the short space of four years, more than fifty books and periodicals were produced by the avant-garde. They not only form landmarks in the history of twentieth-century literature, art and graphic design, but throw light on the development of poetry and art in the rich period preceding the Russian revolutions of 1917. It is only now, when so many of these very rare books have become available in the original, in a collection such as the one owned by the British Library, that a study of the visual side of the material can be attempted.

The writing and its wider, literary context, has already been the subject of other books, so this is an attempt to examine some of the material from another point of view. Nevertheless, however interesting the illustrations and graphic design, neither can be divorced from the writing without a great deal of relevance and meaning being lost. Many of the early books fulfil the hopes of the French artist, Maurice Denis, who had called for a revival of the medieval approach to book design, for the consideration of a page as a totality:

> *Mais l'illustration, c'est la décoration d'un livre!*

and

> *Trouver cette décoration sans servitude du texte, sans exacte correspondance de sujet avec l'écriture; mais plutôt une broderie d'arabesques sur les pages, un accompagnement de lignes expressives.*[1]

Significantly, Denis' theories were collected and re-published in 1912 and a page of the very first Russian futurist poetry book, *Old-time love*, (*Starinnaya lyubov*) [1, 2, 43, 57] bears a curious inscription: writing A Kruchenykh, ornament M Larionov (*sochinenie A Kruchenykh, ukrasheniya M Larionov*) – as though Denis' precept was not far from their minds, for *ornament* is a most unusual word to find in the context.

Many of the artists became writers and made parallel discoveries in words and lines and colours, so that poetry and pictures developed together. Russian futurists made art works, including poems, and then derived theories from them, or, sometimes, wrote theoretical articles and then tried to put the ideas into practice. Sometimes literary ideas influenced the construction of illustrations, often in a literal way, with pictures telling a story as, for instance, in the primitive illustration by the artist Larionov to a poem by Kruchenykh in

3. *Worldbackwards*, 1912: leaf 5, '*Akhme[t]*', illustration to a poem by A. Kruchenykh [colour plate 3] drawn by M. Larionov, lithographed by V. Titaev.

the anthology *Worldbackwards* (*Mirskontsa*) [3 and colour plate 3]. At other times poems followed one pattern and paintings another, though both shared a common foundation, an attempt to create a new kind of art.

In this study, Russian futurists are identified as some among the writers and artists who challenged the older, symbolist generation round about 1910. There were groups with such titles as Ego-futurists, Acmeists, Union of Youth, Hylaeans and later on, Rayists, quarrelling about the nature of their opposition to the past, then joining up in various short-lived alliances. One group, the Acmeists, remained apart and successfully fought the futurist label, which the Ego-futurists adopted late in 1911. Members of the Union of Youth group were accused of futurist leanings, but only when they collaborated with their Hylaean friends in joint activities did they accept the title *futuristy* and use it on posters.

This book is devoted mainly to the Union of Youth and Hylaea groups, together with the Rayist splinter group, because they included the major avant-garde artists of the day whose illustrations and influence helped to determine the character of the publications.

The name Hylaea was chosen to stress a special relationship between southern Russia, the homeland of the Burliuk family who were among the founders of the group, and ancient Greece. Hylaea (*Gileya* in Russian) was that part of the land near the Black Sea which had been settled by the almost mythical forbears of the Greeks, the scene of some of the exploits of Hercules and the country of the Scythians. By emphasising these primitive roots, the group of artists and writers wished to trace their heritage back to a pre-classical settlement and link the present to the ancient past, by-passing the western European classical inheritance by joining up with their own pre-classical primitivism. In this way they both challenged the Russian symbolists with their themes of Apollo and Dionysius and found their own answer to the contemporary French avant-garde interest in non-western and primitive art forms.

A useful account of the remarkably early interest which Russian artists and intellectuals took in indigenous primitive arts and crafts was given by Camilla Gray in her book, *The Great Experiment in Russian Art 1863–1922*.[2] However, both late nineteenth-century artists and those in the World of Art group after them made paintings in which they reconstructed past scenes using folk material in a realist style; they rarely used it to create a new art form. In contrast, Russian futurists recreated past styles in the original spirit of their invention, whether folk broadsheet (in Russia named *lubok*), sign painting, folk song. Byzantine painting or even cave-painting. Each was explored for what it had to give to provide a renewed direct form for painting or poetry.

Whereas an interest in primitive art was crucial to expressionism among the artists of the Brücke group in Germany, Russian futurists avoided this path because of a second interest, French cubism, which they closely linked to the first. They recognised the inventiveness of French art and were frankly influenced by it. Moscow was the first city outside Paris, to boast permanent collections of contemporary art and avant-garde artists were able to see the latest Parisian trends at first hand at the homes of two wealthy merchants, Shchukin and Morozov. Both collectors bought particularly fine examples of work by Matisse and Picasso. By his choice of Picasso's paintings, Shchukin presented Russian artists with a very specialised view of the development of cubism, for in his collection, the majority of Picasso's paintings of 1907–9 are ones based on primitive art. From it, he could be seen to have derived his new, cubist style, characterised by a break with one-point perspective and by the conceptualisation of imagery.

The unique coincidence in Russia of immediate contact with cubism and a rich indigenous primitive past vitalised the artists' and writers' search for an escape, both from the luxuriant hothouse of symbolism and from the anecdotal bias of much nineteenth-century art. Avant-garde painters and poets became concerned with the structure of art, whether visual or literary. The new approach varied from group to group: one of the earliest works of art, remarkable in its originality, was a ten-line poem written by the poet Khlebnikov, first published in 1910 in *Impressionists' Studio* (*Studiya impressionistov*).

Khlebnikov was a brilliant but retiring young poet, respected by all those who became Russian futurists. His poem, 'Incantation by Laughter', '*Zaklyatie smekhom*'[4] consists of variations on the word *smekh*, laughter. Vladimir

4. Impressionists' Studio, 1910: p. 47, detail, poem by V. Khlebnikov: 'Incantation by Laughter' ('Zaklyatie smekhom').

ЗАКЛЯТІЕ СМѢХОМЪ.

Ор. 2.

О, разсмѣйтесь, смѣхачи!
О, засмѣйтесь, смѣхачи!
Что смѣются смѣхами, что смѣянствуютъ смѣяльно,
О, засмѣйтесь усмѣяльно!
О разсмѣшищъ надсмѣяльныхъ—смѣхъ усмѣйныхъ смѣхачей!
О изсмѣйся разсмѣяльно смѣхъ надсмѣйныхъ смѣячей!
Смѣйево, Смѣйево,
Усмѣй, осмѣй, смѣшики, смѣшики,
Смѣюнчики, смѣюнчики.
О, разсмѣйтесь смѣхачи
О, засмѣйтесь смѣхачи!

Викторъ Хлѣбниковъ.

Markov has tried to convey the nuances of the original in his version, part of which reads:

> You who laugh it up and down,
> Laugh along so laughily,
> Laugh it off belaughingly!
> Laughters of the laughing laughniks, overlaugh the laughathons!
> Laughiness of the laughish laughers, counterlaugh the Laughdom's laughs![3]

In Russian, prefixes and suffixes are frequently used to alter the meaning of words. In his poem, by choosing unexpected beginnings and endings, Khlebnikov has given new meanings and suggested new interpretations of a word which denotes action and a particular mood. By restricting the poem to the single word and its transformations he has avoided external references, merely extending the reader's experience of something normally taken for granted. The poem is revolutionary even in Khlebnikov's work, for it has no outside associations, no story.

The poem also raises considerations about the nature of poetic language and it is the interest in the structure and ingredients of art and language which has often earned for the Hylaeans, the Union of Youth and the Rayists, the opprobrious criticism of having created formalist art. Such a generalisation leaves out of account the diversity of approach of members of the different groups and their personal achievements.

Some writers have even found it necessary to excuse Vladimir Mayakovsky's early participation in Hylaea and his futurist activities as a juvenile prank. But although Mayakovsky's mature poetry is revolutionary in a political as well as linguistic way, its roots lie in the formative years of Russian futurism. His creation of a poetic language devoid of bourgeois associations, of gentility and affectation, could not have arisen within any other milieu at that time in Russia. It could only have taken place because a group of friends deliberately set out to sever ties with the encrusted layers of literary and pictorial habits held dear by a particular class of educated public. Neither Mayakovsky nor anyone else, could have achieved the change from art for an élite to art for a new majority, singlehanded. His futurist stage appearances, wearing the famous yellow blouse made specially for him by his mother, his earnest discussions with his older, fellow art student, David Burliuk, who first encouraged and supported his change from painter to poet, the tour of Russian cities with Burliuk and Kamensky, preaching a new approach to art and life, all enabled the young Mayakovsky to experience a rich variety of formative enterprises and invigorating arguments.[4] These allowed him, in turn, to retain his original and challenging approach to life. Above all, the language of his poetry was fed by popular songs, which inspired the poets of the group, as the *lubok* did the painters.

One has only to read the pages of the memoirs of the Italian futurist leader Marinetti, devoted to his visit to Moscow and St Petersburg early in 1914, to see, vividly exposed by the eyes of a rival, the environment which Russian futurist artists and writers were attacking while often still relying on it for financial support. Marinetti's prose is full of mistakes with Russian names and horribly jumbled facts, but it pullulates with the seductions of unheard of indulgence.

At a ball held in his honour in Moscow:

> I agree to lie down on heaped violets surrounded by electric bulbs smothere[ed by] mounds of overheated roses which began to burn
>
> On my back I recite my free verse poem to racing cars although I feel trapped in my rhythms by my position and forced to throw my images up to the ceiling where infinite spirals of smoke mix orange sapphire cobalt sky-blue smells chancing the stench but applauded dazed by my effort and the strong essences I relish the mouth of a woman who creeps up to me to give me advice and that mouth resembles the girl's with the unforgettable walk from the previous night . . .

Besides the beauties, were the objects:

> A theatrical arrangement of objects each in its cradle or nest or shell of petals a jewel hundreds of them under the play of spotlights that dimmed any recollection of the shop windows in Rue de la Paix
>
> Monstrous pink and white pearls with tropical waters swirling around them pearlfishers among slick sharks

and then:

> . . . I abandon myself to the fronds of the potted palms and the large feather fans of the ladies
>
> Without visible bodies we're in an artificial paradise under the sultry hazy air of the tuberoses
>
> I pick my way among the writhing pale forms of beauties lying on the floor while along the walls doze tuxedos and tails like so many copper funeral jars with ivory stoppers . . .[5]

It is a relief to turn from this artificial atmosphere to the accounts of the mundane background of futurist poets and painters – often away in the provinces – given in his memoirs by Benedikt Livshits.[6] In such a milieu, the fresh vulgarity of the sackcloth cover of the first group manifesto *A Slap in the Face of Public Taste* (*Poshchechina obshchestvennomu vkusu*) [colour plate 1e] takes on a new significance. Marinetti's account makes clear why only a dedicated intention to begin again from a new premise could have resulted in Mayakovsky's brilliant achievement and how it could not have been arrived at by himself alone. Without the support and encouragement which the Russian

5. *A Game in Hell*, 1912: hand-written poem by A. Kruchenykh and V. Khlebnikov. Lithographed cover design by N. Goncharova, 18.5 x 14.5 cm.

6. *A Game in Hell*, 1912: p. 5, a devil by N. Goncharova arranged next to verses of the poem by A. Kruchenykh and V. Khlebnikov; lithograph.

7. *A Game in Hell*, 1912: p. 9, two devils by N. Goncharova arranged side by side on leaf without text; lithograph.

8. *A Game in Hell*, 1912: p. 10, N. Goncharova's illustration of the devils' card-game described in the poem; lithograph.

5

6

7

8

futurists gave to each other, any one of them would have been suffocated, or like Marinetti, lionised unbearably.

As it was, by 1915, Mayakovsky was confident enough to write:

> Dear Ladies and dear Gentlemen:
> I – am an impudent fellow who knows no greater pleasure than to throw on a yellow blouse and crash a party of respectable people protecting modesty and dignity under their proper coats, jackets and formal evening dress.
> I – am a cynic – one glance from me will provide your attire with permanent grease spots roughly the size of a dessert plate.
> I – am a cabby who no sooner gains entrance to a drawing room, than the air is filled with words as heavy as axes, words of a profession little equipped for salon dialectics . . .[7]

The inevitable links which were made by critics between the young Russian dissidents, with their manifestos and outrageous publications and exhibitions, and the Italian futurists, pushed the Hylaeans and related groups into an association with a foreign name which many of them regarded as incorrect. There were nevertheless, connections to be made between Italian and Russian futurism: Marinetti had published his first manifesto in 1909, before any of the Russian groups had formed. When the Hylaeans' miscellany, *A Slap in the Face of Public Taste*, went on sale in January 1913, taking its title from the manifesto printed in it, anyone who knew the Italian manifestos must have noted the similarities, as well, it may be hoped, as the differences. It suited the Russians finally to adopt the label *futuristy* during 1913, although many of them continued to use derivations and variations of the Russian language form, *budushchie*, rather than the westernised word.

The arguments about language were crucial for Russian futurists who nearly all belonged to a generation which had grown up at the turn of the century when there was a general movement in favour of the Russian language. It was not uncommon for a law student to be told that he would fail his *viva* if he allowed a single westernised word to pass his lips during his examination. Such nationalism reflected the history of language in Russia itself. It seems extraordinary that as a young man in the early years of the nineteenth century, the greatest Russian poet who ever lived, Pushkin, had admitted that he knew French better than Russian. His efforts to enrich his native language must have inspired the futurist poets in their turn. He advised: 'Listen carefully to the speech of ordinary people. You will be able to learn a lot more from it than from our journals. Read the popular fairy tales to find the real qualities of the Russian language.'[8] It is not surprising that Mayakovsky and the futurists felt them-

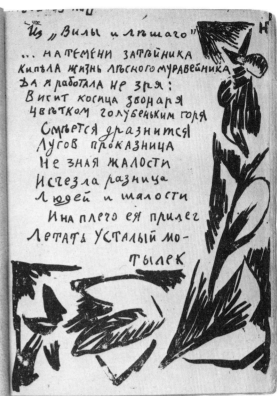

9, 10. *Worldbackwards*, 1912:
leaf 36, N. Goncharova's
illustration of the poem
'Vila and the wood-goblin'
by V. Khlebnikov. Leaf 37,
extract from this poem
with border by N. Goncharova:
lithographs.

selves in rivalry with Pushkin; they, too, were intent on finding a truly Russian modern style, not on making a Russian equivalent to foreign avant-garde styles, in spite of their familiarity with them.

Thus, before the critics dubbed the Hylaeans *futuristy*, Khlebnikov had coined the word *budetlyanin*, by which he meant 'a man of the future'. Instead of heralding the new, mechanised, industrialised world and sweeping away the past wholesale, Russians looked for a 'creation of new things, grown on the magnificent traditions of Russian antiquity'.[9] The books which they published prove the point: the very title *Worldbackwards* (*mirskontsa*), (*mir s kontsa* – world from the end), conveys the antithesis of future-ism. Not only is the end of the world (which may take place at any moment in the future) suggested, but also the beginning of the world, the prehistoric world, long before the civilised world we know had begun. Some illustrations in the book show that artists were prepared to go right back to the Stone Age in order to begin a new way of making art, not by depicting imaginary scenes, but by copying the basic strokes which man had scratched on caves millenia ago [60]. The anthology includes an extract from a poem by Khebnikov entitled 'Vila and the woodgoblin' ('*Vila i leshii*') [9, 10] which Nataliya Goncharova illustrated in a suitably ugly, primitive way. The result was closer to the drawings made *by* children than the editions of legends published *for* children with colourful illustrations by World of Art artists at the turn of the century.

However, roots in the past would not alone have resulted in a reform of poetic language and innovations in the field of painting and sculpture. The admixture which was most fertile for Russian futurists was cubism, which, even more than the manifestos of Italian futurists, helped to restructure creative language. Because so many Russian futurists approached writing from a background of visual art training, they turned their attention to adapting cubism to words. Even Khlebnikov, who had not trained as an artist, was not content to describe or evoke the past. In his poems he treated words in a way analogous to the way cubists treated form. Instead of lines, planes and colours, arranged in an unexpected order on canvas in order to present a fuller interpretation of reality, Khlebnikov 'dislocated' the words and phrases of his poems. He segmented and rearranged the parts of language, inventing plausible prefixes and suffixes for existing roots or building new meanings with real beginnings and endings added to imaginary roots. He did this to give a fuller meaning to poetry, to break language free from time-worn convention.

In description, this procedure sounds remarkably abstract, but what was crucial about the choice of cubism as a model by Russian futurists was that in itself, cubism was never non-figurative, it was intrinsically linked to the world of reality. Indeed, the most striking feature of the style invented by Picasso and Braque in Paris (and named '*cubisme*' in mid-1909 by the critic Louis Vauxcelles) was its reliance on simple, immediately accessible subject matter, which the artists proceeded ruthlessly to analyse. A person painted in a cubist portrait is not generally detached from his environment, he shares the same lines and colours. The portrait is not a likeness in the accepted sense, the whole canvas is subjected to dissection into faceted planes to convey the sculptured figure and the space which surrounds it. As the viewer's eye roves carefully over the painting, signs of more than one nose, or ear or mouth appear, the sitter shifts, the musical instrument is broken, as if seen simultaneously from several viewpoints by the artist.

Gradually, Picasso and Braque invented devices for simplifying their paintings: in 1912 they began to put 'reality' back in the form of glued-on shapes: printed oil-cloth to represent chair-caning, newspaper cut into shapes to make 'real' planes and add a subverted meaning by the surviving printed words. Composition became far simpler: cut shapes were laid on a white or coloured ground and shading and additional marks added to create representations of 'reality' to accompany the 'real' elements. Cubism can be seen as a new kind of realism.

Any present-day attempt to put into a few words the characteristics of Picasso and Braque's cubist painting is inevitably coloured with hindsight. For the Russian futurists, who used the term cubo-futurist to describe some of their paintings, cubism was a theory expounded by two French artists, Gleizes and

Metzinger, in a book which was translated twice into Russian in 1913;[10] it was examples of cubist paintings which they saw in private collections, in exhibitions; it was photographs sold by the Parisian art dealer, Kahnweiler, brought back by travellers from France; it was articles and photographs published in French and German art journals and in exhibition catalogues. To a writer or artist in Russia, cubism was not the movement revealed by any present-day description, but some of the details combined with extra interpretations.

For example, David Burliuk regarded *faktura*, roughly translated as 'texture', as immensely important and all the poets thought that what they termed *sdvig*, shift, was a key concept. Again, David Burliuk insisted that the cube itself was a vital part of cubism, a three-dimensional, solid object, which was seen by another Russian futurist, Mikhail Matyushin, as part of a system for portraying a fourth dimension.

Russian artists soon adopted the most important formal cubist invention made by Picasso and Braque. This was to compose by manipulating shapes on a surface (canvas or paper) so that the resulting picture forsook the renaissance canons of perspective. A new reality of the picture itself (as an object) was established to replace the convention of an illusion of external reality. Colours and lines and texture had a new, self-contained meaning, which poets quickly sought for words. Kruchenykh asked for a word 'broader than sense'; Khlebnikov invented a 'transrational' language which he called *zaum*; Mayakovsky wrote a poem 'From street to street' (*'Iz ulitsy v ulitsu'*) which, although unique in his output, the artist Malevich considered the most successful experiment in 'versified cubism'.[11] It is composed of words and phrases arranged vertically so that they read nearly the same both backwards and forwards.

Originally, neither poets nor painters intended a literature or art that would be devoid of meaning. *Zaum* was to be a universal language, overcoming the boundaries of conventional words. Lines and colours would not copy what is seen by the eye or camera, they would be used for themselves in a new form of signification. But this proved almost more difficult than a new way with words. It took much longer to create abstraction in art than in poetry.

This is particularly surprising, since the Russian artist, Vasily Kandinsky (who had settled in Munich) exhibited his remarkably abstract looking 'Compositions' and 'Improvisations' in Russian art exhibitions before he showed them elsewhere. Strangely, they were described by the futurists as 'free drawing' and hardly imitated at all. Kandinsky's text, *Über das Geistige in der Kunst*, so crucial for the development of abstraction in England, was made known in St Petersburg in shorter form, as a lecture in December 1911.[12] Though discussed at length at the time, it took its place simply as one among many lectures and publications which, over the next few years, led gradually to the challenge by the Russian avant-garde of all previously accepted ideas about art and literature.

Finally, at the end of 1915, geometric, coloured non-figurative forms were advanced as a system named suprematism by the painter, Kazimir Malevich [79, 80], in the same year that wire, metal, wood and other materials were given freely controlled form, in 'counter-relief' sculptures invented by Vladimir Tatlin.[13] This was two years after an artist turned writer, Aleksei Kruchenykh, had first published his *zaum* poem of made-up words, *'Dir bul shchyl'*.[14]

The books, journals, plays which comprise Russian futurist publications elucidate the gradual pathway which led to these formidable inventions in literature and art.

2

POETS AND PAINTERS –
A CHRONOLOGY

It is clear from the previous chapter that the scope of this book is restricted to the beginnings of Russian futurism, to the years of exploration in words and visual forms. They correspond to the period of outstanding graphic invention, when publications showed the greatest originality in design. Unlike any other modern movement, Russian futurism is largely self-documented, as the medium chosen by the protagonists was the printed book.

The complexity of the movement is revealed by the bewildering number of different approaches to book design and content, adopted by the groups of writers and artists [11, 12]. Not only do the book-covers show startling inventiveness [colour plate 1] but the contents are found to include an enormous variety of illustrative matter, sometimes with little differentiation being made at first glance between the approach to writing and drawing. Yet a

11. *Explodity*, 1913: leaf 3, *zaum*
writing and decoration
by A. Kruchenykh; lithograph.

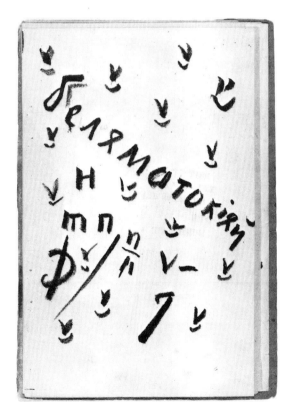

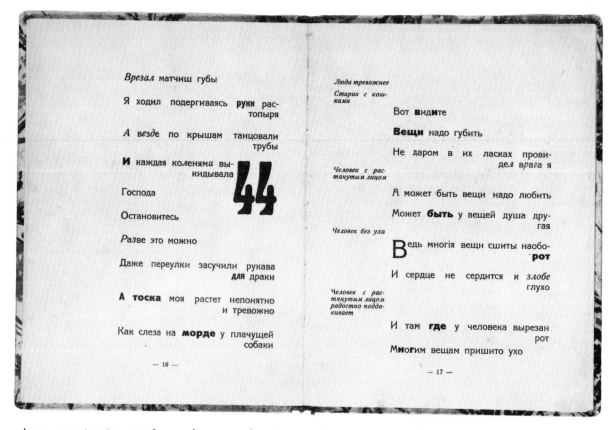

Left page (16):

Врезал матчиш губы

Я ходил подергиваясь **руки** рас-
топыря

А *везде* по крышам танцовали
трубы

И каждая колен*ями* вы-
кидывала **44**

Господа

Остановитесь

Разве это можно

Даже переулки засучили рукава
для драки

А тоска моя растет непонятно
и тревожно

Как слеза на **морде** у плачущей
собаки

— 16 —

Right page (17):

Люди тревожнее

*Старик с кош-
ками*

Вот **видите**

Вещи надо губить

Не даром в их ласках прови-
дел в*рага* я

*Человек с рас-
тянутым лицом*

А может быть вещи надо любить

Может **быть** у вещей душа дру-
гая

Человек без уха

Ведь многія вещи сшиты наобо-
рот

И сердце не сердится к *злобе*
глухо

*Человек с рас-
тянутым лицом
радостно подда-
кивает*

И там **где** у человека вырезан
рот

Мн**о**гим вещам пришито ухо

— 17 —

12. *'Vladimir Mayakovsky'
– A Tragedy*, 1914: pp. 16, 17
designed by D. and V. Burliuk;
the names of Mayakovsky's
characters are shown in italics
in the margin.

closer examination reinforces the point that Russian futurism is merely a convenient label by which to identify writers and artists who were united only in opposition to the immediate past and to those of their contemporaries who were not as radical as themselves. Furthermore, the books elucidate alliances and allegiances within the movement, which, if separately chronicled, prove extremely complicated.

The material is most usefully classified according to the changing loyalties of artists and writers who continued the practice of adopting colourful names to identify a 'new trend' in art. The key role played by artists in the development of all the varying approaches labelled futurist in 1913, means that the most convenient names to use are often those of exhibiting societies.

Between 1906 and 1910 some of these artists had shown their work in Moscow and St Petersburg in a series of exhibitions with titles such as Stephanos, Golden Fleece, Triangle, and the more staidly named Moscow Artists Association. In the case of Golden Fleece (in Moscow) the title was that of a journal as well as an exhibiting society, so it was not surprising when, after an exhibition in St Petersburg with the title 'Impressionists', a journal was published entitled *Impressionists' Studio* (*Studiya impressionistov*) [32]. Yet by the time it came out before the end of March 1910, most of the protagonists in St Petersburg had joined a new association, the Union of Youth, formally registered in February. Unlike many of its predecessors the Union of Youth was long-lived and played a vital role in fostering the ideas of its members, not only in exhibitions, but in publications, meetings and sponsorship of plays.

After the first exhibition of the Union of Youth was held in March, a second book was published in St Petersburg. It was called *A Trap for Judges* (*Sadok sudei*) [colour plate 1b] and was intended to be more shocking than *Impressionists' Studio*. It included poetry by Vasily Kamensky, Velimir Khlebnikov, Elena Guro, David Burliuk and his brother Nikolai, while another brother, Vladimir, provided portraits of most of the contributors [42]. *A Trap for Judges* set a precedent by linking contributors from the Moscow and St Petersburg avant-garde. The two books brought together so many writers, some of them practising artists, who were to play a leading role in later developments, that the origin of Russian futurism is usually found in them.

Among the contributors to both books, Victor Khlebnikov, who took the more Russian name, Velimir, was an outstandingly gifted poet and was the most influential of the group of writers. He had been discovered by Vasily Kamensky two years before, when he had shyly submitted poetry to a magazine which Kamensky was editing.[1] Khlebnikov was enrolled as a student of biology, Eastern languages and Sanskrit at the University of St Petersburg. Already aged twenty-five in 1910, he had previously been a student of mathematics at the University of Kazan. In St Petersburg he was spending more time on writing than on his studies. He had regularly attended evenings held by Vyacheslav Ivanov, a major symbolist poet, but when these transferred to the editorial offices of a new journal, *Apollon*, Khlebnikov's writing clearly no longer fitted in. Kamensky had introduced Khlebnikov to Nikolai Kulbin, who edited *Impressionists' Studio*, and to Mikhail Matyushin and his wife, the poet Elena Guro; Matyushin and Kamensky were among the initiators of *A Trap for Judges*.

Khlebnikov's poem, 'Incantation by Laughter' [4] was an early example of his experiments with language. Its inclusion in Kulbin's book was later on regarded as one of the first manifestations of futurism. But although Khlebnikov had proved himself the most creative new Russian poet, being a retiring, absent-minded scholar, he was totally unsuited to the role of leader and remained very much a background figure.

Although spring 1910 may be seen as a useful date to begin a discussion of Russian futurism, because of the two books and the formation of the Union of Youth, there was little further publishing activity until 1912. However, later in 1910, some of the artists from Moscow who had taken part in the first Union of Youth exhibition formed a new exhibiting society which they called the Knave of Diamonds. The name was chosen by Mikhail Larionov, who was granted his diploma at the Moscow School of Painting, Sculpture and Architecture in September,[2] after spending the summer in southern Russia with his fellow-student, David Burliuk.

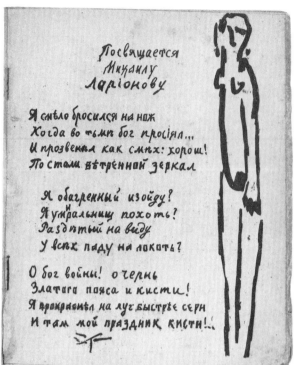

Shortly after the first Knave of Diamonds exhibition was held in Moscow, early in 1911, Larionov was dissatisfied with the majority of artists whose work he regarded as too closely following the French post-impressionist painter, Paul Cézanne. By March he had decided on a new title for a breakaway group, Donkey's Tail, from the story told in the newspapers about a group of French artists who had tied a brush to a donkey's tail and submitted to an exhibition the daubs of colour the angry animal had made on a canvas. As well as Larionov and Nataliya Goncharova, the Donkey's Tail group included two other artists who were to play an important role, Kazimir Malevich and Vladimir Tatlin.

Among those who did not join Larionov was David Burliuk, who later claimed to be the father of Russian futurism. In December 1911, while he and his brothers were preparing for the opening of the second Knave of Diamonds exhibition, they were trying to find a distinguishing name for themselves. This fact and the eventual choice of the name Hylaea is recorded in the memoirs of the poet Benedikt Livshits, who stayed with the Burliuks at their home in southern Russia for the Christmas vacation.

Although Livshits wrote his recollections of the period nearly twenty years later, *The One and a Half-Eyed Archer (Polutoraglazyi strelets)*[3] – alluding to the one-eyed David Burliuk – provides the most lucid account of the period, seen from the slightly biased point of view of a founder member of the Hylaea group. Because of this, he accorded David Burliuk virtually all the credit for the inception of Russian futurism. It is true that by the time of Livshits' visit to the home of the Burliuks, David had already made what was to prove a decisive

13. *Half-alive*, 1913: hand-written poem by A. Kruchenykh. Lithographed cover design by M. Larionov.

14, 15. *Half-alive*, 1913: leaf 1, with Kruchenykh's dedication to Larionov, whose drawing of a nude accompanies the text; by leaf 11, Larionov's figure has become much less readable; lithographs.

16. *Half-alive*, 1913: leaf 17, full-page figure by M. Larionov, constructed with calligraphic strokes to match the violence of Kruchenykh's poem; lithograph.

...зилый блёдный смрадный
Вошел во а? как в дом
...оял там воздух чадный
Меня обдали кипятком

И тотчас в ногти мне впилися
Кормили свежими червями
В глаза глядели и вилися
...тя отвислыми ушами

Их палец тщился начертать
Мои земныя пять имен
Но легче .....коготь поломать
Чем отгадать как я клеймен

Тут я узрел родное пленя
И сны ощупал на яву
Носил давно я пятки бремя
И прокричал я сквозь гом : живу!

intervention in the movement, by befriending a new fellow-student at the Moscow School of Painting, Sculpture and Architecture and persuading him that his talents lay in poetry rather than in painting. This young student was Vladimir Mayakovsky, without whose genius Russian futurism might well have been forgotten. Simply by discovering Mayakovsky and helping him financially in his earliest years as a poet, David Burliuk could have earned the title of father of the movement. The claim can also be upheld on the grounds that in 1910 at twenty-eight he was the oldest member of the active group. He was well-read in modern German and French literature and an experienced artist, having studied in Munich and Paris as well as Odessa.

Another important role which David Burliuk assumed, was disseminating information about new art movements, both by giving lectures illustrated with lantern-slides and by writing articles for catalogues and books. He had contributed an introductory article to the catalogue of a major international avant-garde exhibition held in Odessa in September 1910, the second Salon organised by a wealthy sculptor and art patron, Vladimir Izdebsky. Izdebsky had so much admired the paintings sent from Munich to his first exhibition by Kandinsky, that he exhibited fifty-three in his second Salon and printed a woodcut by him on the cover of the catalogue.[4] As a result of the exhibition, Burliuk was invited by Kandinsky to contribute articles about Russian avant-garde painting to the catalogue of his breakaway exhibiting group in Munich and then to his almanac *Der Blaue Reiter*.[5] In turn, Kandinsky and his friends sent paintings to the first two Knave of Diamonds exhibitions in Moscow.

Burliuk's knowledge of modern art movements must have been extremely up-to-date, for the second Knave of Diamonds exhibition, held in January 1912, included not only paintings sent from Munich, but some by members of the German Brücke group, while from Paris came work by Robert Delaunay, Henri Matisse and Fernand Léger, as well as from Picasso.

During the spring, David Burliuk gave two lectures on cubism and planned a polemical publication, which the Knave of Diamonds was to finance. He went abroad in May and came back determined to rival the almanac *Der Blaue Reiter*,[5] which had emerged from the printers while he was in Germany. When he arrived back in Moscow, he wrote anxiously to Nikolai Kulbin in St Petersburg enquiring whether Kulbin could find contributors for his forthcoming book, now definitely planned for autumn publication.[6] But as the Union of Youth had brought out the first number of their own journal in March and were by then preparing a second, talent in St Petersburg was otherwise engaged and Burliuk received no articles or poems from the capital. Perhaps writers in St Petersburg were not yet convinced by this Moscow avant-garde, or its ability to produce a book, though they were soon to be persuaded.

By the middle of October, Burliuk's book was pre-empted by two members of the rival Moscow Donkey's Tail group, Larionov and Goncharova, with Aleksei Kruchenykh, who had recently given up art for writing. They produced two outstanding lithographed, handwritten and illustrated poetry books, with the participation of Khlebnikov. These were *Old-time Love* (*Starinnaya lyubov*) [1, 2] and *A Game in Hell* (*Igra v adu*) [5–8]. This annoyed the Knave of Diamonds intensely, probably because Kruchenykh was a contributor to the book they had promised to sponsor and his new alliance with the Donkey's Tail artists appeared as a betrayal. So they withdrew their support for Burliuk, whose book entitled *A Slap in the Face of Public Taste* (*Poshchechina obshchestvennomu vkusu*) was finally registered early in January, from the same publishers[7] (Kuzmin and Dolinsky) who had by now produced a third book for Kruchenykh – *Worldbackwards* (*Mirskontsa*).

In retrospect, among the most controversial inclusions in *A Slap*, other than the manifesto from which it took its title, were the Russian versions of four little prose poems by Kandinsky. The heading acknowledges that they are: 'four little tales from his book *Klänge* (published by R. Piper and Co. Munich)'. Kandinsky's name thus became linked with the first group manifesto to be published in Russia and Livshits described him as an 'occasional member of our group'. Kandinsky spent part of the autumn of 1912 in Russia so it is probable that he agreed to the inclusion of his work in a book still sponsored by the Knave of Diamonds, to whose exhibitions he had contributed. But once Burliuk lost this backer and added a manifesto (written in December) that was clearly related to Italian futurist prototypes, the book must have greatly changed character and

Видѣть.

Синее, Синее поднималось, поднималось и падало.
Острое, Тонкое свистѣло и втыкалось, но не протыкало.
Во всѣх углах загремѣло.
Густокоричневое повисло будто на всѣ времена.
      Будто. Будто.
Шире разставь руки.
      Шире. Шире.
И лицо твое прикрой красным платком.
И может быть оно еще вовсе не сдвинулось:
        сдвинулся только ты сам.
Бѣлый скачок за бѣлым скачком.
И за этим бѣлым скачком опять бѣлый скачок.
И в этом бѣлом скачкѣ бѣлый скачок. В каждом
         бѣлом скачкѣ бѣлый скачок.
Вот это-то и плохо, что ты не видишь мутное:
        в мутном-то оно и сидит.

Отсюда все и начинается . . . .
. . . . Треснуло . . . .

(Страничка изъ „Klänge" 1913 г.)

17. *Artist's text*, 1918
by V. V. Kandinsky: p. 5,
a page from *Klänge* 1913;
this poem – 'To See' –
by Kandinsky, was included in
A Slap in the Face
of Public Taste in December 1912
without the vignette.

annoyed Kandinsky. Later he had no wish to be associated with such an outrageous enterprise and wrote a letter to a newspaper expressing his annoyance.[8] The publication of *A Slap* marked the end of interaction between Munich and Moscow at this time, though it is not without significance that when he returned to Russia, Kandinsky's *Artist's Text* (*Tekst khudozhnika*) of 1918, opened with a revised version of one of these poems [17].[9]

Perhaps one reason why Burliuk received the title 'father of Russian futurism' was because his first book was presented as deliberately antagonistic, with its aggressive title and manifesto. In contrast, Kruchenykh's first three remarkable books – *Old-time Love*, *A Game in Hell* and *Worldbackwards* – were presented to the public, not as examples of any movement or tendency, but simply as themselves, a new kind of book with a new approach to graphic design, illustration and poetry.

Aleksei Kruchenykh was two years younger than Burliuk, of peasant origin and had never travelled abroad. He had attended art school in Odessa and qualified as a teacher of graphic art in 1906. He published a lithographic album, *All Kherson in Caricatures, Cartoons and Portraits* (*Ves Kherson v karikaturakh, sharzhakh i portretakh*) in 1910, by which time he was living in Moscow. In his reminiscences[10] he glosses over these early years, but the winter of 1912–13 was marked by the publication of six books for which he was responsible. As a group, they remained unsurpassed as 'artists' books'.

Credit must be given to the role played by the publishers, Georgy Kuzmin and Sergei Dolinsky. They are described by Vladimir Markov as a pilot and a composer while Nikolai Khardzhiev calls them an aviator and young poet. As well as Kruchenykh's books, they published two by David Burliuk and a collection of poems by Mayakovsky between October 1912 and June 1913. This independent patronage and encouragement relieved both Kruchenykh and afterwards Burliuk of the necessity of being tied to the policy of an exhibiting group as sponsor. It freed them from any *a priori* programmatic commitments and helps to account for the originality of each of the books. The publishers evidently made no demands on the authors and allowed them to experiment in very different ways. It is unlikely that Kuzmin and Dolinsky saw themselves as the first publishers of a specific new movement in literature and art, but rather as sponsors of contemporary Moscow writers and artists. Of the books they brought out, only *A Slap* included a manifesto – its emphasis as much on the present as the past or future: 'Only we are the face of our time.'

The winter of 1912–13 was characterised by a fragile unity between the factions of the avant-garde, in art as well as literature. Although Burliuk had failed to attract contributors from St Petersburg for his book, he and his brother united with Larionov's group to exhibit at a fourth Union of Youth exhibition which opened in the capital on 4 December. The cover of the catalogue carries a mistake in dating which has proved very unfortunate: the printers wrote 4 December–10 January 1912 instead of 4 December 1912–10 January 1913. After 1932, when two Soviet historians misinterpreted the date and said that Mayakovsky had shown his first painting in December 1911, a false impression of the development of avant-garde art was built up, until they admitted the mistake in a book published in Moscow in 1970.[11]

Seen in its correct chronology, the exhibition catalogue corroborates the evidence of an illustrated book, published in St Petersburg in February which once again united members of the Union of Youth with the Moscow Hylaea faction and Larionov's group. It was called *A Trap for Judges 2* (*Sadok sudei 2*) and was published by Matyushin under his own imprint, *Zhuravl* [colour plate 1a]. A manifesto was included, signed by the Moscow signatories of *A Slap*, with Benedikt Livshits, Nikolai Burliuk, Matyushin's wife Elena Guro and her sister Ekaterina Nizen. They described themselves as 'new people of a new life'.

During the spring of 1913, joint activities were arranged by the Union of Youth and Hylaea in St Petersburg, culminating in March with the publication of a third number of the journal of the Union of Youth, with a new format. The fact that the Union invited Larionov and the Hylaeans to come separately to the capital is a reminder that, within Moscow, Larionov was still a rival of the Burliuks. In spite of the fact that he and Goncharova collaborated with Kruchenykh on three further books of poetry, they were planning a new ambitious exhibition which they called Target, again in rivalry with a third Knave of Diamonds show, to which David Burliuk remained loyal.

In the end Larionov did not go to St Petersburg to give a lecture on the new style which he had been developing, but a small book, illustrated with reproductions of work by himself and Goncharova [18] went on sale during the

18. Reproduction of 'Rayist Construction, 1912' by N. Goncharova, included in *Rayism*, 1913, and *Donkey's Tail and Target*, 1913.

last week of April. In it he set out his new theory under the Russian title *Luchizm*, which has usually been translated as 'rayonnism'. Although this is a correct French translation of *luchizm*, an exact English equivalent is ray-ism. Presumably because the style was first noticed in western Europe in the French press, the word *rayonnisme* was simply taken over by English-speaking historians who did not realise the meaning of the Russian original.

The publication of *Rayism* (*Luchizm*) marked the beginning of a separatist position which Larionov consolidated during the summer, when he seems to have been determined to promote himself and Goncharova as the leading avant-garde artists in Moscow. Their biography was written (under the pseudonym Eli Eganbyuri) by a new friend, Ilya Zdanevich, the brother of a painter who had taken part in Larionov's exhibitions.[12] Another book, *Donkey's Tail and Target* (*Oslinyi khvost i mishen*), had a frontispiece photograph of his immediate group posed at the Target exhibition [19]. In the book, which came out before the end

19. *Donkey's Tail and Target*, 1913: frontispiece photograph showing M. Larionov (left), N. Goncharova (third from right); behind the group are 'The Four Seasons' and a Venus painting by Larionov.

of July, copies of some of the lithographs he had made for Kruchenykh were pasted in to one article as illustrations. Likewise, the biography *Nataliya Goncharova and Mikhail Larionov* included other examples of lithographs originally made by them for Kruchenykh's poems. The period of collaboration had ended with three books published in February: *Hermits* (*Pustynniki*) [20, 21], *Half-alive* (*Poluzhivoi*) [13–16] and *Pomade* (*Pomada*) [colour plates 4, 5];

1a. *A Trap for Judges 2* (*Sadok sudei 2*), 1913; **b.** *A Trap for Judges* (*Sadok sudei*), 1910; **c.** *The Croaked Moon* (*Dokhlaya luna*), 1913; **d.** *Explodity* (*Vzorval*), 2nd edition, 1914, lithograph by O. Rozanova; **e.** *A Slap in the Face of Public Taste* (*Poshchechina obshchestvennomu vkusu*), 1913; **f.** *Te li le*, A. Kruchenykh, V. Khlebnikov, 1914; **g.** *Four Birds* (*Chetyre ptitsy*), 1916, drawing by A. Lentulov; **h.** *A Game in Hell* (*Igra v adu*) A. Kruchenykh, V. Khlebnikov, 1912, lithograph by N. Goncharova; **i.** *Transrationals* (*Zaumniki*), A. Kruchenykh, 1922, lino-cut by A. Rodchenko.

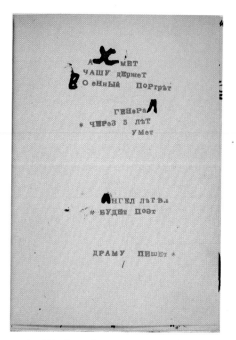

2. *Worldbackwards* (*Mirskontsa*), A. Kruchenykh,
V. Khlebnikov, 1912. Collage flower
on cover by N. Goncharova. Title label glued-on.

3. *Worldbackwards* (*Mirskontsa*), leaf 6, Rubber-
stamped poem by A. Kruchenykh with letters
added by stencil or potato-cut. 18.1 x 13 cm.

4. *Pomade* (*Pomada*), A. Kruchenykh, 1913.
Shiny, red paper cover with glued-on title label
and lithograph by M. Larionov.

5. *Pomade* (*Pomada*). Lithograph by M. Larionov,
'Lady with a hat', glued on to gold-leaf paper.
14.9 x 10.5 cm.

6 and **7**. *Gardeners over the Vines* (*Vertogradari nad lozami*), 1913.
Double-page coloured lithographs on the stone by N. Goncharova inserted between
Sergei Bobrov's poems 'Life' (*Zhizn*) and 'Stories' (*Skazki*), pp. 38–9 and 78–9. 17.6 x 23 cm.

8. *First Journal of Russian Futurists 1–2 (Pervyi zhurnal russkikh futuristov 1–2)*, 1914.
Vladimir Burliuk lithograph printed in three colours opp. p. 12.

9. *Milk of Mares (Moloko kobylits)*, 1914.
Vladimir Burliuk drawing in three colours
opp. p. 16. 19.2 × 12.5 cm.

10. *The Croaked Moon (Dokhlaya luna)*, 1913.
Frontispiece etching by David Burliuk
(bound in this way up) cut crooked. 18.8–19.5 × 15.2 cm.

11. *The Bung (Zatychka)*, 1913.
Vladimir Burliuk double-page lithograph with hand-colouring.
19.8 x 25.5 cm.

12. *Te li le*, 1914. Poem by A. Kruchenykh,
drawing by O. Rozanova,
reproduced by hectography. 22 x 15.5 cm.

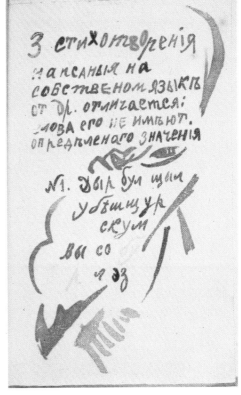

13. *Te li le.* Text by A. Kruchenykh
with his *zaum* poem '*Dyr bul shchyl*' below;
decoration by O. Rozanova. 22.2 x 14.5 cm.

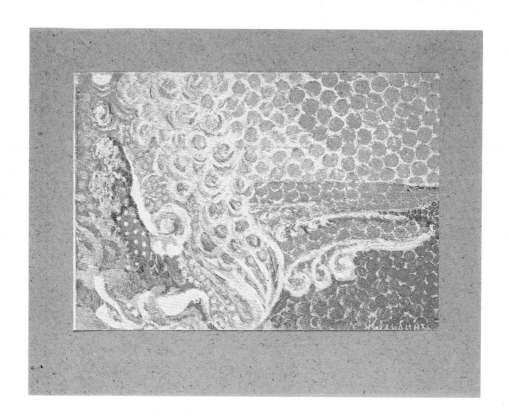

14 and **15.** *Impressionists' Studio (Studiya impressionistov)*, 1910.
Colour plates illustrating Evreinov's monodrama 'The Performance of Love'. 14:
N. I. Kulbin, opp. p. 96; 15: L. F. Shmit-Ryzhova, (1909), opp. p. 80.

16. A. Lentulov unrealised set design (1914) for '"V. Mayakovsky" – A Tragedy',
plate from *Graphic Art (Graf. iskusstvo)* tipped in to
The Vernal Forwarding Agency of the Muses (Vesennee kontragentstvo muz), 1916.

17. *Le-Dantyu as a Beacon (LidantYU fAram)*,
Iliazd (I Zdanevich), 1923.
Collage cover by N. Granovsky.

18. *The Spent Sun (Solntse na izlete)*, K. Bolshakov, 1916.
Cover lithograph by El Lissitzky (strengthened at edges).

19. *Piglets (Porosyata)* Zina V., A. Kruchenykh,
1913. Cover. K. Malevich, 'Peasant woman'.
Lithograph. 9.6 x 14.5 cm.

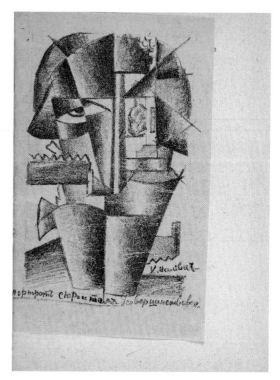

20. K. Malevich, 'Portrait of a Builder Completed'.
Lithograph. 17.5 x 11.2. Tipped in to *Piglets*, 1913,
between pp. 12–13.

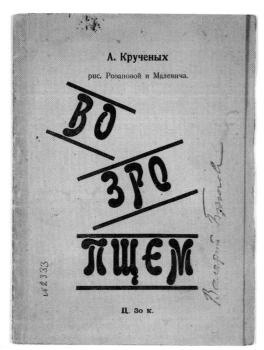

21. *Let's Grumble* (*Vozropshchem*), A. Kruchenykh,
1913. Cover of British Library copy
showing Valery Bryusov's library stamp.

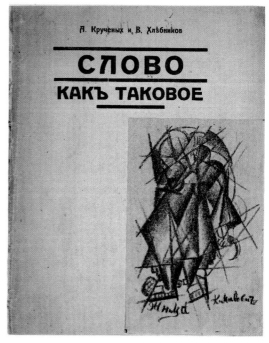

22. *The Word as Such* (*Slovo kak takovoe*),
A. Kruchenykh, V. Khlebnikov, 1913. Cover.
K. Malevich: 'Reaper'. Lithograph. 14.5 x 9.5 cm.

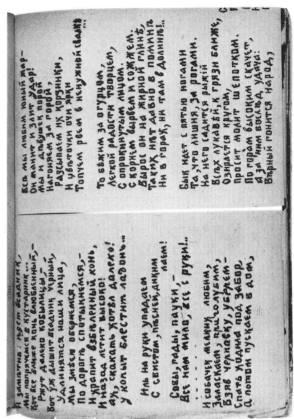

20, 21. *Hermits*, 1913: leaf 2, a hermit by N. Goncharova illustrating the poem by A. Kruchenykh. Leaf 8 shows the unusual arrangement of the text, which appears to have been intended for a book of smaller format; lithographs.

Larionov and Goncharova's contribution to *A Trap for Judges 2* marked the last time their work was printed with that of the Union of Youth or Hylaea [62, 63].

Other changes of allegiance took place at the end of March 1913, for although one of the contributors to Larionov's Target exhibition was Kazimir Malevich, he was not included in the group photograph taken there [19]. During the spring it must have become increasingly clear that the relationship his work had shared with Goncharova's was no longer so close, and indeed, even before the Target exhibition opened, he went to St Petersburg with members of the Hylaea group and spoke at a meeting with the Union of Youth. Early in the summer he began to contribute lithographs to the new books published by Kruchenykh.

By this time Kruchenykh had moved to St Petersburg where he established his own publishing imprint, *EUY*.[13] As well as including lithographs by Malevich in his books during the remainder of the year, he relied on the collaboration of Nikolai Kulbin and Olga Rozanova. Dr Nikolai Kulbin was an amateur artist, a military doctor by profession and a constant member and supporter of the avant-garde. (He had edited *Impressionists' Studio* and organised a number of exhibitions before the founding of the Union of Youth.) Kruchenykh apparently moved to the capital on account of Olga Rozanova, who played an increasingly important role as collaborator on his books; by 1915 and 1916 these were made by their exclusive partnership, almost entirely by hand.

Kruchenykh's role in Russian futurism was altered by his move. Later in the year, in *The Word as Such* (*Slovo kak takovoe*), under the heading 'About artistic production', he outlined the way he viewed the avant-garde approach in writing and art, describing two camps: in Moscow, David Burliuk, Mayakovsky, Livshits and Kazimir Malevich; in St Petersburg, Khlebnikov, himself, Elena Guro[14] and the artists Vladimir Burliuk and Olga Rozanova. But as he now relied on the inclusion of lithographs by Malevich in his own books published in St Petersburg and himself contributed to those which David Burliuk published in Moscow, he provided a link between the two groups.

Connections between Moscow and St Petersburg were sustained when Kruchenykh, Matyushin and Malevich held what was grandly termed the First All-Russian Congress of Singers of the Future (Poet-futurists) at Matyushin's Finnish dacha in July.[15] Although the three of them were planning a futurist opera, they expected the forthcoming futurist theatre programme to include a tragedy which Mayakovsky was already writing in Moscow.

During the summer of 1913, David Burliuk planned and printed further books in south Russia, which came out later that autumn and winter, distinguished for the first time by the word *futenisty* as well as Hylaea, printed on the covers [colour plate 1c]. In Moscow, Burliuk planned the 'First Evening of Russian Futurist Wordmakers' in October, to include members from St Petersburg.[16] Preparations went ahead for two performances each, of the futurist opera 'Victory over the Sun' and '"Vladimir Mayakovsky" – a Tragedy'. Burliuk was involved, for a lithograph he had contributed to *A Trap for Judges 2* was used on the poster.[17] The productions were organised by the Union of Youth in St Petersburg for the beginning of December, coinciding with their fifth exhibition.[18] A Moscow production of Mayakovsky's tragedy was planned in 1914, but did not take place, although the artist Aristarkh Lentulov designed a set for it [colour plate 16].

The Union of Youth in St Petersburg was much stronger than Hylaea was in Moscow. A problem in Moscow was the split in the avant-garde caused by Larionov's insistence on taking a separate line. Burliuk had attempted to strengthen Hylaea by writing to Livshits during the summer and urging him to come and 'be our Marinetti'. But Livshits was engaged in his compulsory military service and could not take an active part in a polemical movement. Still determined to broaden his group, Burliuk persuaded Kamensky to participate.

Vasily Kamensky had shown early literary leanings, but had given up writing after he had achieved little success with a novel which had been published in 1910.[19] He took up flying and became a stunt pilot, travelling round Europe visiting air fairs, but after a crash he gave up flying. Kamensky agreed to join David Burliuk and Mayakovsky on a futurist tour of Russia during winter of 1913–14 and the three visited many cities, putting on evenings of poetry-reading with lectures on the new movement in art. There is a delightful story of children in one town, chanting 'the footballers are coming', mistaking *futuristy* for *futbolisty*.

This winter tour was the first directly proselytising activity which any of the Russians had attempted outside Moscow and St Petersburg. During the summer, rival groups had paraded in the streets of Moscow with their faces painted with motifs, as in the descriptions of ancient Aztecs. At Christmas, Larionov explained why in a newspaper article: 'The new life requires a new community and a new way of propagation',[20] a view which is surprisingly close to Kruchenykh. A sense of urgency to exploit the uniqueness of Russian futurism was furthermore engendered by the forthcoming visit of Marinetti to Russia.

Marinetti visited Russia only once, in January 1914, and the arrival of the leader of Italian futurists was greeted with mixed feelings by the *futuristy* of all groups. David Burliuk, Mayakovsky and Kamensky were away from Moscow on their tour; Larionov published a letter in the press, encouraging Russians to throw eggs at Marinetti, Malevich replied with a plea for reasonableness; at a meeting which Marinetti was to address in St Petersburg, Khlebnikov forgot his usual shyness and distributed leaflets to the audience, inveighing against foreigners.

In St Petersburg, one of the oldest members of the avant-garde, Nikolai Kulbin, organised a dinner for Marinetti, attended by Livshits. In *The One and a Half-Eyed Archer* he records an argument he had with Marinetti on this occasion which gives the clearest account of the fundamental differences of approach between Italian and Russian futurists.[21]

Visual proof of the total gulf between the two is to be found in the books discussed on Marinetti's visit. Marinetti declaimed his *Zang Tumb Tuum*,[22] Kulbin showed him the latest St Petersburg book, *Te li le* by Kruchenykh and Khlebnikov [colour plates 1f, 12, 13]. The Russian book has a nonsense title like the Italian – both were looking for an irrational art – but unlike the Italian, the Russian title has no onomatopaeic references. Marinetti's book was typeset, albeit with typographical innovations; Kruchenykh's was handwritten with decoration by Kulbin and Rozanova, reproduced in colour by a primitive gelatine process called hectography. Even if the language experiments were lost on Marinetti, he praised the originality of the book which was totally unlike anything being produced in Italy.

Although this is the only record of Marinetti's comment on a Russian futurist publication, it is likely that on his visit he saw another book, also about to go on sale. This was *Futurists: Roaring Parnassus (Futuristy: rykayushchii Parnas)*, a miscellany published in St Petersburg with a frontispiece manifesto. It fulfilled a similar function to *A Trap for Judges 2* of almost exactly a year before, by uniting members of Hylaea with the Union of Youth. The contributors once again reflected changes and new alliances. The book was financed by Kseniya

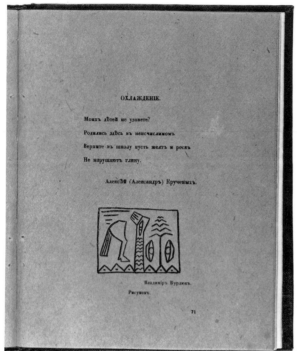

Boguslavskaya, wife of Ivan Puni (Jean Pougny) – both artists had recently returned from Paris where they had been living.[23] Among the Moscow artists, only the Burliuks were represented, but drawings by Pavel Filonov appeared in print for the first time [23].

Filonov was a member of the Union of Youth who had made the costumes and one set for the recent production of Mayakovsky's tragedy. Undoubtedly an

22, 23. *Roaring Parnassus*, 1914:
p. 71, poem by A. Kruchenykh
printed above a drawing
by Vladimir Burliuk.
P. 33, drawing by Pavel Filonov.

24. *A Selection of Poems 1907–14*,
by V. Khlebnikov. 8 and 9 of
16 leaves of illustrations and
handwriting by Pavel Filonov.

artist of extraordinary originality, he occupied a somewhat isolated position in the avant-garde. He seems to have been close to Khlebnikov and provided illustrations and handwritten pages [24] as a supplement to the *Selection of Poems 1907–14* (*Izbornik stikhov 1907–14 s poslesloviem rechyara*) by Khlebnikov, published in March. Just as Khlebnikov cannot be contained as a writer within the confines of a single movement, as an artist, Filonov was equally isolated and more unreasonably misunderstood, even during this period. According to Professor Markov, Khlebnikov considered a later book by Filonov the best work about the war. This was *Sermon-Chant about Universal Sprouting* (*Propeven o prorosli mirovoi*) (of 1915) which is also an exceptional example of very high quality printing [25].

    Roaring Parnassus and the contemporary *Milk of Mares* (*Moloko kobylits*) (published by David Burliuk), both included a new literary contributor, Igor Severyanin, a well-established poet, who had founded Ego-futurism in October 1911.[24] His first manifesto had appeared a year before Burliuk's, but, in spite of the early adoption of the name 'futurist', Ego-futurist publications have even less connection with the Italian movement than the Hylaeans. Anticipating

25. *A Sermon-Chant about Universal Sprouting*, 1915: written and illustrated by Pavel Filonov. Pp. 8–9, tipped-in drawing, printed in sepia, opposite part of 'The Song of Ivan the Steward' ('*Pesnya o Vanke Klyuchnike*').

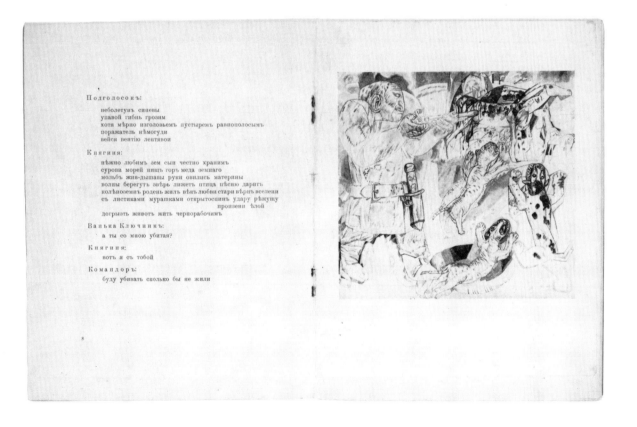

Kruchenykh's first books, Severyanin had produced a series of miscellanies and a newspaper, but, although their work is clearly worth studying for its literary merits, Ego-futurists did not share the broader basis of their rivals, given by the union of artists and writers in Hylaea and the Union of Youth. Only a year after founding it, Severyanin left the Ego-futurist movement, declaring that he was 'attracted by the primitive'. His position was close enough to the symbolists' to earn their praise and he became a popular figure, holding poetry readings in the style of a decadent. Kulbin was apparently responsible for Severyanin's rather surprising alliance with the Hylaeans. Early in 1914 on a tour of the Crimea Severyanin read his poetry with Burliuk and Mayakovsky. In retrospect, it is not possible to judge whether the unusually aggressive manifesto in *Roaring Parnassus* was due to the new signatory, Severyanin, or simply to a determination among Russian futurists to prove their credibility at the time of Marinetti's visit. The book title was entered in *Knizhnaya letopis*[25] the week after the end of his visit; Livshits' story that only ten copies were saved from the printers may be fictitious, for only when a book had been passed by the censor was it registered in the official weekly bibliography.

The opening manifesto in *Roaring Parnassus* ends with the sentence: 'We have dropped the incidental labels of "ego" and "cubo" and have formed a literary company of futurists.' This sweeping statement caused more uproar than previous manifestos, but the clause proved correct when the *First Journal of Russian Futurists 1–2 (Pervyi zhurnal russkikh futuristov 1–2)* appeared with its impressive list of contributors. The editor was Kamensky, the publisher David Burliuk and there was participation (actual and prospective) of: Mayakovsky, Livshits, Kulbin, Kruchenykh, Matyushin and also Igor Severyanin, Vadim Shershenevich, Konstantin Bolshakov and even Sergei Tretyakov.

Of the new contributors, Shershenevich had a great deal to do with the *Journal*, since Burliuk and his friends were away on their futurist tour. As a member of a short-lived group named the Mezzanine of Poetry, in 1913 Shershenevich had tried to set out an account of futurism from their point of view in a book called *Futurism without a mask (Futurizm bez maski)*.[26] Bolshakov was a fellow member of the Mezzanine, so it is rather surprising that Larionov and Goncharova remained aloof from the *Journal* as they had illustrated a book of his poems, *Le Futur*, a few months earlier. In fact, given the wide spectrum of opinion among the literary contributors, it seems strange that the artists listed were so few; an unexpected inclusion was the French artist, Fernand Léger, but this was in all probability due to the participation of Aleksandra Ekster. She played an active part in the books produced early in 1914, though in a new way: photographic reproductions of her paintings were included in the *Journal* and in *The Milk of Mares*. Aleksandra Ekster was the wife of a wealthy lawyer from Kiev and was able to live for half of the year in Italy or France where she studied with prominent artists, so she acted as a remarkable messenger bringing information to Moscow about the latest trends in Europe.[27]

During the winter of 1913–14 many of the old rivalries were still apparent in the field of the arts. In November 1913, the Union of Youth exhibition had drawn David Burliuk, Malevich, Tatlin and Ekster from Moscow, while in January, a fourth Knave of Diamonds exhibition included Malevich and Ekster. As before, Larionov and Goncharova remained apart, organising their own show, simply called No 4. But in this exhibition there was a new development: Kamensky was invited to exhibit a number of his 'ferro-concrete' poems [55]. He had already published some in the *Journal* and also in two remarkable books, printed on the reverse side of brightly patterned wallpaper.[28]

1914 marked the beginning of a greater awareness among Russian artists of their international standing. Some had already exhibited in Kandinsky's

26. *Explodity*, 1913: *zaum* poems and text by A. Kruchenykh. Lithographed cover design by N. Kulbin. 17.7 x 12.2 cm. (torn and restored lower right-hand corner).

exhibitions in Munich and Larionov and Goncharova had sent work to Roger Fry's second Post-impressionist exhibition in London[29] but, following Marinetti's attempts to draw Russians into a futurist alliance with the Italians, Kulbin, Rozanova and Ekster contributed to a futurist exhibition in April in Rome.[30] Interestingly, Kulbin sent a drawing which had been used as a cover lithograph for Kruchenykh's book, *Explodity* (*Vzorval*), the previous summer, chosen, perhaps, because it closely resembles a tumultuous futurist gathering [26]. The three artists were not a representative sample of Russian futurists, but Malevich, in spite of having defended Marinetti shortly before his arrival in Russia, sent work to Paris, to the Salon des Indépendants, rather than to Rome.[31] In May, Larionov and Goncharova held an exhibition in a dealer's gallery in Paris,[32] on the occasion of Diaghilev's production of 'Le Coq d'Or', for which Goncharova had designed the sets and costumes. Larionov had publicly

27. N. Goncharova: 'Angels and Aeroplanes', 32.5 x 24 cm. No. 10 of 14 lithographs included in her portfolio entitled *War*, 1914.

attacked Marinetti's visit, yet, in June 1914, notice was given in the Italian futurist journal *Lacerba* that he and Goncharova would shortly appear as contributors.[33]

The outbreak of war in August not only delayed further numbers of *Lacerba*, so that a drawing by Larionov was not finally included until a year later,[34] but it substantially changed the futurist scene in Russia. Larionov was drafted and wounded, and late in 1915 he and Goncharova made their way to Switzerland where they joined Diaghilev in what proved a fruitful partnership. Larionov designed a remarkable ballet, '*Contes Russes*', combining the past and present in a most typically Russian futurist idiom. Before they left Russia, Goncharova made a portfolio of lithographs about war, subtitled 'Mystical images of war' [27] and lithographs for various books; both artists continued their book illustrations in Paris, where they settled after the war, joining activities variously labelled dada or surrealist, very much in the spirit of their futurist ventures in Russia.

David Burliuk and Mayakovsky had been expelled from art school because of their futurist tours, but, in compensation, it must be said that these had proved lucrative. Later in 1914, Mayakovsky began to be paid regularly as a journalist and was able to repay some of David Burliuk's earlier generosity by giving him financial help which he needed, for after the outbreak of war there was no longer public interest in futurist demonstrations.

However, futurist activity did not entirely cease: in March 1915, a year after the *First Journal of Russian Futurists*, a new magazine, *The Archer* (*Strelets*), came out. It had a widened range of contributors, for as well as Hylaea it included writers of reputation, such as Aleksandr Blok, Mikhail Kuzmin and Aleksei Remizov, prominent members of the symbolist generation. Its publication was celebrated at the Stray Dog, a night club in St Petersburg, with a party at which an event took place marking a new era of respectability for the futurists.[35] Maxim Gorky was present and uttered the words: 'They've got something!' referring to the futurists. He followed it up by publishing an explanation, singling out Severyanin, Mayakovsky, Burliuk and Kamensky: 'What they need is not abuse, but simply a humane approach, because even in their shouts and invectives there is something good.'

In a way, this recognition signified a death knell for those concerned. Nearly all of the publications in which they took part in 1915 and 1916 reveal compromises which diluted the original spirit of Hylaea. An exception of December 1915 was a polemical attempt at a new journal made by David Burliuk and Mayakovsky called *Took: a futurists' drum* (*Vzyal: baraban futuristov*). Its large new format with a drab dark paper cover bearing the single word *VZYAL* (Took) [28] in bold type was reminiscent of the vorticists' *Blast*. The connection is established by an interview with Ezra Pound about the English

28. *Took – A Futurists' Drum*, 1915:
David Burliuk, V. Mayakovsky,
V. Khlebnikov and V. Shklovsky –
who recalled that the letters
were set in a wooden type
used for posters and afterwards
had to be hand painted
with Chinese ink,
(*O Mayakovskom*, 1940).
Black lettering
on dark grey, woodchip paper.

vorticists which had been included in *The Archer*; El Lissitzky spoke later of the influence in Russia of the typographical innovations in *Blast*.[36]

El Lissitzky himself returned to Russia from Germany at the outbreak of war; his connection with the Moscow avant-garde is marked at this time by a cover design he made in 1916 for *The Spent Sun* (*Solntse na izlete*)[37] by Konstantin Bolshakov [colour plate 18]. Lissitzky's design is seen to be much closer to contemporary work by Ekster, such as her two beautiful etchings [29] in Ivan Aksenov's *Weak Foundations* (*Neuvazhitelnye osnovaniya*)[38] than to the position which he adopted while working at the art school in Vitebsk with Malevich in 1919, which led to his remarkable experiments in book design in the early 1920s.

Malevich had given an account of the extreme stance, which he named suprematism, in a book published by November 1916.[39] A full explanation was needed to support the non-figurative, geometric paintings he had first exhibited almost a year before in Petrograd at an exhibition named 'Zero-ten, the Last Futurist Exhibition', where a pamphlet had been on sale.[40] There, across the corner of the room reserved for his paintings, hung the 'Black Square' painting,[41] which he reproduced as a lithograph in his book [80]. For some, even of the avant-garde, the ruthless reduction seemed to foretell the death of art; for the artist it was rather a new beginning, a *tabula rasa*, a zero, from which a

29. *Weak Foundations*,
1916:
poems by I. A. Aksenov.
Original etching
by Aleksandra Ekster
tipped-in
between pp. 24–5,
34.4 x 26 cm.

new art could arise: a literal victory over the sun, over past forms. Finally, pictorial art could have its own *zaum*, 'language of the stars'.

For Malevich's friend Kruchenykh, who was noticeably absent from most futurist activities after the outbreak of war, the paintings were such a revelation that in his next book words seemed virtually unnecessary. *Universal war* (*Vselenskaya voina*) consists of collages by Rozanova, cut into abstract shapes which float on the deep blue pages, unsupported by text.[42] Shortly afterwards, Kruchenykh left the capital for Tiflis where he remained for three years.

Futurism had a brief revival there, for Tiflis avoided the revolution and became part of the Soviet Union in 1920. Kruchenykh joined Zdanevich, earlier a member of Larionov's group, and they held evenings of poetry readings and lectures. They named a group – 41° – which was also a publishing enterprise: *Learn art* (*Uchites khudogi*) is an example of their new, hand-produced books [30]. Zdanevich began to write plays, but the culmination of his activity in that field came after he had settled in Paris where he adopted a new pseudonym, Iliazd, under which he published a play, *Le-Dantyu as a Beacon* (*lidantYU fAram*), which forms a summing up of earlier Russian futurist and *zaum* ideas [31, 39 and colour plate 17].

Kruchenykh himself returned to Moscow and took part in the uneasy years when futurism was still a title for the avant-garde, though his book,

30. *Learn Art*, 1917:
handwritten poems
by A. Kruchenykh.
Lithograph pasted on to cover
of stiff, brown paper.
23.5 x 19 cm.

Transrationals (Zaumniki) of 1922 is distinguished by a cover design by
Rodchenko which in retrospect must be called constructivist [colour plate 1i].
The borders between futurism and constructivism are blurred in much the same
way as those between dada and surrealism in the West. Yet it is totally
consistent with the advent of a new kind of society and political system that
futurism should have led to constructivism, an attempt to subordinate
individuality for the benefit of the masses, whereas in Europe, the dada
movement, which is closer to Russian futurism than Italian, should have made
way for a movement which extolled individuality in its extreme.

3

THEATRE

Among the poems, manifestos, articles and illustrations which comprise the majority of Russian futurist publications under discussion, there are dramatic works, some of which, taken together, encapsulate the changes in avant-garde approach between 1910 and 1923.

    The earliest, printed in Nikolai Kulbin's book, *Impressionists' Studio*, (*Studiya impressionistov*) is a symbolist monodrama, 'The Performance of Love', written by Nikolai Evreinov and accompanied by colour illustrations [colour plates 14, 15]. In contrast are a futurist opera and tragedy, which were performed in St Petersburg at the height of futurist activity in December 1913 and published as separate books soon afterwards. The opera was *Victory over the Sun* (*Pobeda nad solntsem*) written by Kruchenykh with prologue by Khlebnikov, music by

31. *Le-Dantyu as a Beacon*, 1923: pp. 52–3, text and typography by Ilya Zdanevich, printed in Paris – a development from the Burliuks' typography of *'Vladimir Mayakovsky'* – *A Tragedy*, 1914 [12].

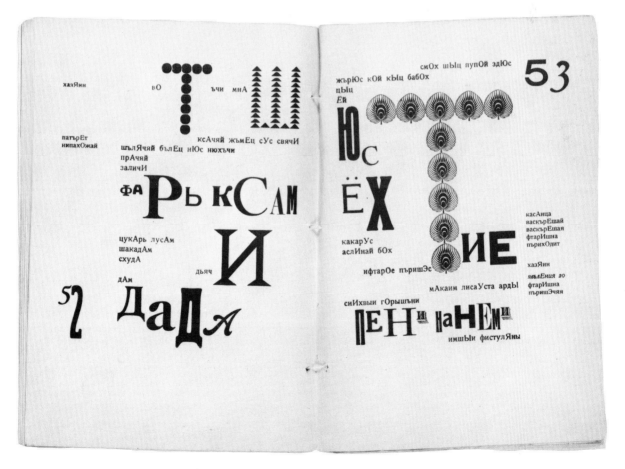

Matyushin and sets and costumes by Malevich. The text was published a few weeks after the production. The tragedy was written by Mayakovsky and entitled 'Vladimir Mayakovsky' – a Tragedy ('Vladimir Mayakovsky' – Tragediya); it was registered at the very end of March 1914. Another dramatic work is Le-Dantyu as a Beacon (lidantYU fAram) which was printed in Paris after the author, Ilya Zdanevich, moved there, though he may have written the play in Russia [colour plate 17]. Le-Dantyu as a Beacon is to be considered as a summing up of graphic design, ideas about staging and a culmination of Kruchenykh's zaum language, treated in a masterly way by Zdanevich, who took the name Iliazd for the publication of the play. In the West it seems to belong more to the dada movement than to futurism, because it was published in 1923 by which time constructivism had overtaken the earlier movement in graphic design in Soviet Russia. Zdanevich may have intended a dada connection for page fifty-two [31] includes the word 'dada'.

'The Performance of Love' marks the end of one epoch and the beginning of a new. The Russian title, 'Predstavlenie lyubvi' has recently been translated as 'The Presentation of Love' by John Bowlt[1] and also as 'The Representation of Love' by Oliver Sayler in a very interesting eyewitness account of Russian theatrical activity in his book, The Russian Theatre.[2] However, the specialised theatrical meaning of the Russian word which Evreinov chose, predstavlenie, is 'performance' which I have used because it gives a clearer suggestion of the erotic overtones of the play.

As a dramatic work 'The Performance of Love' is more introverted than Maeterlinck's symbolist plays and although Evreinov described it as impressionist, his use of the word has nothing to do with the French impressionist painters. He described the term in his introduction: '. . . in art we must absolutely try to attain variety in unity achieving in this way an easily conceived simplicity and thus a whole impression – an aesthetic pledge – of the significant.'[3]

Evreinov was a theatre director in the line of Stanislavsky and Meyerhold whom he had succeeded at Vera Komissarzhevskaya's Dramatic Theatre in St Petersburg.[4] His theories must be seen in the then recent tradition of Russian theatre, of plays staged not for commercial success, but for their value as an art form.

Reform of the theatre had begun in Russia in the 1880s when a rich Moscow merchant, Mamontov, had staged productions in his own home, inviting prominent artists to come and design the scenery. From then on, many artists were involved with stage design, which was considered of prime importance in any production. Artists of the World of Art group worked on the decor and costumes for an extraordinary series of productions staged in 1907–8 during Evreinov's season of Old-time Theatre. This was a revival of medieval forms

32. *Impressionists' Studio*, 1910, edited by N. I. Kulbin. Title-page by A. A. Andreev (Dunichev) with the word *Studiya* composed from figures from Evreinov's 'Old-time' theatre. 'The Triangle' was used by Kulbin as the title of an exhibition in 1910.

which he explored during research into the history of drama. The title page of *Impressionists' Studio* carries lettering formed from cut-out figures of actors dressed in medieval costumes in the style of these experiments [32].

In 1908, Evreinov set out his own theory of monodrama in a lecture, publishing it as *An Introduction to Monodrama* in 1909.[5] After the publication of 'The Performance of Love' he developed the principles further and in 1912 he went so far as to locate the action of 'The Greenroom of the Soul'[6] inside the chest of the human body.

As published, with its symbolist-style illustrations 'The Performance of Love' seems totally an end in itself and an unlikely starting point for a new approach to theatre. Yet because they were available in a book well-known to Kruchenykh and Mayakovsky, Evreinov's ideas repay consideration as much for their influence on futurist theatre as for their intrinsic interest.

In his introduction Evreinov explained:

> Monodrama forces every one of the spectators to enter the situation of the acting character, to live his life, that is to say

to feel as he does and through illusion to think as he does and as it were, above all to see and to hear the same things as the acting character.[7]

and:

. . . in the perfect drama, becoming 'my own drama', only one acting character in the strict meaning of the word is possible, only one subject of action is thinkable . . . the spectator of the monodrama perceives the other participants in the drama only as they are reflected in the subject of action, and consequently, their experiences having no independent significance are presented on the stage as being important only in so far as the perceiving 'I' of the subject of action is projected in them.[8]

So each of the characters beyond the central one, the 'I', is to be interpreted as subject to him, even though the illustration by Lyudmila Shmit-Rizhova [colour plate 15], shows the 'She! She!' character as existing independently. One of Kulbin's illustrations is intended as a set design, for three sides are framed by a proscenium arch; it depicts 'I' sitting on a hillside beside the shoreline of a sea and is the most theatrically possible of the five.[9] Another [colour plate 14] illustrates a particular speech in the play:

Is it you I am embracing? . . . Yes? . . . Is your hair per-fumed? . . . Do I hear your breath? . . . Yours? . . . Yes? . . . Yes, it is you, you! . . . You! . . . No, do not resist! . . . Listen, listen . . . (I still say something, but what, – I do not understand, I do not know, I do not hear. In the dark fog, still, there is distinct green gold . . . Either it curls or freezes on the spot! . . . Envelopes, shrivels . . . Dies in a minute of darkness, comes to life again, grows pink, purple, makes odd designs, tinkles with opalescent murkiness, wafts an unearthly charm, rains, becomes an ocean, warms with colours).[10]

Kulbin has represented coloured waves, curling round the barely visible forms of Evreinov's introverted eroticism. The erotic content is ambivalent when submerged in such colour and light.

Introspection carried to such extremes is peculiar to Evreinov himself, but the descriptions of monodrama quoted above fit Mayakovsky's tragedy in a remarkable way. There is only one character in the tragedy, that is, only one who is recognisable as a character, namely Vladimir Mayakovsky himself; all

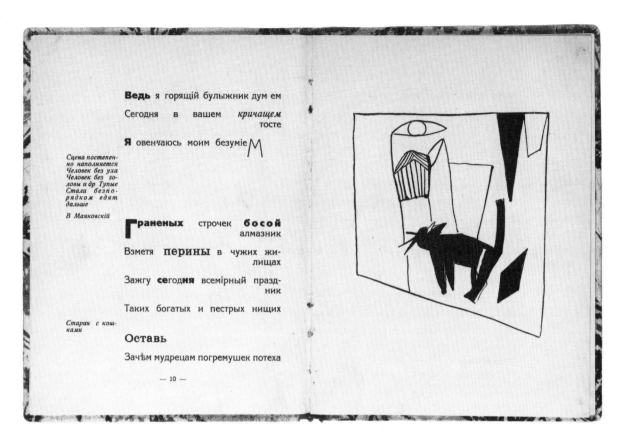

33. 'Vladimir Mayakovsky' – A Tragedy, 1914: p. 10, with (David) Burliuk's drawing of The Old-man with Cats.

the other parts are figments of the hero's imagination. But unlike the idealised figures imagined by Kulbin and Shmit-Rizhova, the illustrations by the Burliuks for 'Vladimir Mayakovsky' – a Tragedy show them as fragments dominated by their characteristics [33, 38].

The tragedy was, of course, performed and a contemporary drawing of the first scene shows the hero, played by Mayakovsky himself, standing in the centre of the stage dressed in the futurist yellow blouse in which he usually appeared in public; he is raised on a white plinth with his characters round him.[11] They are reduced to puppets, each actor dominated by his attribute: the Man with a stretched face; the Man without an ear; the Old man with cats. They have become cardboard doll-like figures, their costumes painted by Pavel Filonov on canvas stretched on figure frames which the actors pushed in front of them.

Once again Evreinov's theories are relevant:

> ... we cannot in monodrama accord to the other participants in the drama the significance of acting characters in the strict sense of the word ... How they look by themselves remains concealed; we shall see them only as they appear to the acting character. It is quite possible that the latter will ascribe to them attributes which they would not have in our eyes.[12]

But Mayakovsky interpreted Evreinov's ideas in a new and alarming way. In place of the narcissistic embrace in 'The Performance of Love' Mayakovsky peoples his stage with a terrible love:

> do not soil the ends of your hearts with anger
> you as my children
> I will teach unbendingly and sternly
> for all you people are only the little bells
> on [God's] cap[13]

What kind of love? The Man with two kisses tells in the second act:

> a big dirty man
> was given two kisses
> the man was clumsy
> did not know what to do with them
> where to put them

But

> ...the man was
> cold and had holes in the soles of his shoes ovals
> he chose the bigger kiss
> and put it on his foot like a galosh

The man's fingers and then his feet were bitten by the frost, so he decided he did not need the kisses and threw them into the road

> and suddenly
> ears grew on the kiss
> he began to fidget
> and in a thin little voice he cried
> I want Mummy
> the man took fright
> he wrapped the trembling little body with the rags of his
>   soul
> took it away to put in a pale blue frame

This gives a fearsome twist to Evreinov's theory of monodrama – suddenly the attributes of the hero's character have taken on their own life, frightening the character who, we realise, has described *himself* as a 'big dirty man'. He now tells that one of his attributes, the little kiss, grew fat and big on his sofa at home, so much so, that the man hung himself. He grants his own epilogue to the story:

> and while he was hanging repulsive and pathetic
> in boudoirs women factories not needing smoke and
>   chimneys

> were throwing out kisses by the millions
> all sorts
> big one and small ones
> with the fleshy levers of smacking lips[14]

Mayakovsky's characters may be subservient to himself, even speaking his own words both as author and hero, but they are detached in the form of a recounted story of which the earthiness and even bawdiness is in total contrast to Evreinov's 'Performance of Love'.

Therefore Mayakovsky's tragedy is not usually related to Evreinov's work but to another stage production, Shakespeare's 'Hamlet', as directed by Edward Gordon Craig at the Moscow Arts Theatre in 1911.[15] In her memoirs, Marussia Burliuk described how she and David took Mayakovsky to see the production: 'And when Mayakovsky saw "Hamlet" with us, even then the plan of his own production began to grow in his mind.'[16] It is easy to imagine how enthralled the nineteen-year-old art student must have been.

There are connections between Mayakovsky's tragedy and this production of 'Hamlet'. Gordon Craig, whose theories about the drama were just as pronounced as Evreinov's, insisted that Hamlet must remain on the stage throughout the performance because the whole action depended on the hero. Craig reduced a number of the characters to ciphers: for instance, in the Players' scene the king and queen were clothed in gold robes which spread out in front of them and the courtiers were arranged so that they literally emerged through holes in the train, becoming part of the royal pair.

Gordon Craig himself was not satisfied with the production and even Stanislavsky expressed reservations about it. Nonetheless, 'Hamlet' was given many performances and represented the practical application of the ideas of one of the great theoreticians of the time. Furthermore, unlike Evreinov's 'Performance of Love' and its introduction, 'Hamlet' had all the power of a realised stage production with stage effects happening in front of the audience and not just in the imagination of a reader.

Of the performance Marussia Burliuk remembered:

> Instead of decorations, movable screens of various sizes and cubes were used. To portray the beauty and the richness of the palace Craig had some of the cubes covered with gold paper. In other scenes they appeared only gray. On the stage there were no doors, windows, or furniture. Everything [depended on] the imagination of an onlooker.[17]

Craig had developed the use of screens in order to create a three-dimensional stage space avoiding decorated backdrops, wings and arches which he regarded as giving a false illusion of 'painted reality', a two-dimensional setting clashing with the three-dimensional actors. He arranged the groupings of the screens to suggest changed locations, originally intending the scene changes to take place in full view of the audience. Colour and atmosphere were provided largely by lighting and costumes. It is unlikely that Mayakovsky would have known about the technical difficulties, such as the various unsuccessful attempts Craig had made with metal, wood and even cork, before plain canvas screens were decided on to solve the problem of weight. Thus, any influence of the setting on the tragedy, and on the opera which was produced at the same time, must have been from 'Hamlet' as performed, rather than from rejected ideas.

In fact, elaborate staging had been intended for Mayakovsky's tragedy. The financier of the Union of Youth, which sponsored the futurist theatrical productions in December 1913, recalled:

> The three-dimensional sets (with numerous ladders, bridges and passages) originally intended by Shkolnik were not feasible in those days, so the designer went to the other extreme and contented himself with two picturesque backdrops on which were painted two excellent urbanistic landscapes, in form and content little connected with the text of the tragedy.[18]

The sketch of the first act shows a rather wild painting of a town on a backdrop which was smaller than the stage space, giving it more the air of a screen than of a conventional, illusionistic setting. The single screen may have also been suggested by those used by the Italian futurists on the stage – which, in turn, had in some way been copied by the Russian futurists in their 'Evenings', the first of which had been held in Moscow in October 1913.[19]

Mayakovsky's tragedy and the opera 'Victory over the Sun' were staged as examples of a 'theatre of the future-man' which had been announced in a declaration in July 1913 by the First All-Russian Congress of Singers of the Future (Poet-Futurists).[20] This elaborate-sounding title described a meeting of Kruchenykh (self-styled chairman) and Malevich (secretary) with Matyushin at his dacha in Finland. Meanwhile in Moscow, Mayakovsky was apparently already writing his tragedy.

There were many examples of avant-garde approaches to theatre and design for anyone planning a revolutionary production – some of which have already been suggested. The idea of a theatre of the future-man could be quite independent of any Italian futurist manifesto. Yet the quotation, 'We proclaim as an absolute necessity that the composer must be the author of a dramatic or tragic poem that he has set to music', seems quite likely to have triggered off a response, especially in Matyushin, who composed the music for 'Victory over

34. *The Three*, 1913: prelude to the opera 'Victory over the Sun', text by A. Kruchenykh, music by M. Matyushin, on reverse of p. 41.

the Sun'. It is, however, a misquotation found not in the original manifesto of Italian futurist musicians of 1911, but in a footnote by Kandinsky to his article 'On Stage Composition' published in *Der Blaue Reiter*.[21]

This clue reveals yet further resources on which those concerned with a theatre of the future might draw and when the opening bars of 'Victory over the Sun' appeared in print in *The Three* (*Troe*) in September 1913 an instant link was established with the opening words of Kandinsky's 'Yellow Sound', printed in the almanac over a year before. 'Yellow Sound' begins:

> *Prelude*
> A few indistinct chords from the orchestra
> CURTAIN
> On the stage it is dark-blue dawn, which at first is whitish and later becomes intense dark blue.[22]

Below the opening bars of music by Matyushin for 'Victory over the Sun' are printed '*budetlyanskiya*' musical notes and the words: 'Transition with blue and black.' [34] Following Kandinsky's example, colour was evidently connected with sound from the first. The very full stage directions to 'Yellow Sound' can be read as a lighting score:

> Soon the music starts, first at a high pitch. Then suddenly and quickly dropping lower. At the same time the backdrop turns dark blue (simultaneously with the music) with wide black edges (like a picture)...[23]

These effects in themselves may derive from the use of colour pioneered on the stage in Munich by Rudolph Steiner. The schismatic group of German theosophists of which he was the leader began in 1910 to stage plays with such titles as 'The Portal of Initiation' in which very elaborate colour changes were used to enhance the mood and degree of participation of the audience. Indeed, the Steiner plays were specifically intended as a form of religious exercise for the audience, which was more like a congregation than a usual theatre audience.[24]

It is tempting to link these ideas, with which Kandinsky was familiar, with the Russian theatre of the future-man, who in Kruchenykh's words, was trying to lead the audience to higher intuition, the state of mind 'broader than sense'. Khlebnikov's prologue to the opera began: 'People! Those who are born but have not yet died. Hurry up and go to the *sozertsog* or *sozertsavel*'[25] using neologisms formed from the Russian words for 'contemplation' and 'spectacle.' Livshits, in his memoirs, describes the Luna Park Theatre at the beginning of the opera as a 'black abyss'.[26] The theme of the opera was the victory over the source of life for the three-dimensional man on earth, so that he might glimpse a new life. Evreinov had written in his introduction to monodrama:

> We often say 'Yes' instead of 'No' when the sun shines, but it shines sometimes in our soul more brilliantly than in the sky, and this sunshine, not less than the real sunshine, may lighten up with royal comfort our miserable setting. I may utter my 'Yes' or 'No' in deep meditation...[27]

Kandinsky had also been drawn to Evreinov's ideas, for they were originally to have been included in the Munich almanac. Franz Marc sent the publishers a provisional table of contents of the first number in September 1911 which included 'Monodrama – Yevreinoff'.[28]

But there was yet another precedent for the authors of the opera, as well as for Kandinsky, included in *Der Blaue Reiter*. This was an article describing 'Prometheus', the most ambitious composition by the contemporary Russian composer, Scriabin, who combined colour with sound. 'Prometheus' (subtitled 'The Poem of Fire') was written for orchestra and chorus with the accompaniment of colour. Included in the article was the description:

> In a blue-lilac twilight the mystical harmony sounds . . .

and

> According to the composer's idea the whole hall is filled
> with blinding rays at the same time that all the forces of the
> orchestra and chorus are mobilised . . .[29]

which sounds remarkably close to the 'blades of light' which shone so brightly
in Malevich's lighting for 'Victory over the Sun'. The artificial light from the
spotlights was used in what Livshits described as 'a night of the creation of
the world'[30] (a birth of the new light and sound for the man-of-the-future).

Of all the descriptions of new staging ideas – in which the Russian theatre
abounded – the futurist opera sounds one of the most intriguing. From all
accounts lighting played a very important part in creating the dramatic effect.
The Union of Youth hired the Luna Park Theatre in Petersburg, which was
equipped with very modern lighting, for four nights at the beginning of
December, for the performances of the opera and the tragedy. According to
Livshits the spotlights in 'Victory over the Sun' were used in a new and daring
way. He compared Malevich's use of lighting for the two performances, to a
production which many of his readers could remember, which suggests that the
change in theatre lighting round about 1913 had already taken place when the
Vera Komissarzhevskaya Dramatic Theatre had been done up and renamed
Luna Park.[31] Hand-controlled spotlights had been used for some years in the
theatre, but it was not until 1913 that the modern system of console-controlled
lighting became available. Instead of each spot having to be controlled by a
different technician, making the effects unreliable – they could be changed from
a single central source; the long-desired effect of lighting orchestration could be
properly realised for the first time.

Livshits describes how the 'tentacles of the spotlights' cut up the bodies of the
actors into geometric sections. This could have been achieved convincingly only
by using coloured spotlights projected from the sides of the stage, by which
means, the white parts of the costumes would take colour from the lights, while
the yellows, blues, reds and other colours would be distorted or even swallowed.
The existing designs for the costumes show many with large white areas, with
only the arms, legs, even heads picked out in colour.[32] The absorption of similar
colours by the coloured spots and the gift of colour to the white areas would
produce the effect which Livshits described: the figures 'broken up by the blades
of light . . . alternately lose arms, legs, head.'[33] Because the three primary colours
of stage lighting are red, green and blue (not the red, yellow and blue of
pigments), the colour loss could only be achieved by mixed colours, which
probably accounts for the overpainting of areas on the costume designs, some of
which Zheverzheev, secretary of the Union of Youth, collected, and are now in
the theatre museum in Leningrad.

Although the visual side of the opera was evidently so arresting, Kruchenykh, the author, seems to have been determined that the words should not disappear. On stage, however, they may have been lost in the rendering by amateur singers, who had been chosen so that they should not have preconceived ideas to spoil the unusualness of the performance. Some time between 20 December 1913 and 1 January 1914 an edition of a thousand copies of the text came out. Unfortunately the available translations of 'Victory over the Sun' in English and in French do not seem able to convey any of the punning and double meanings which must be there for the Russian seeker for a new language [35].[34]

In *The Three* Kruchenykh had written: 'Before us there was no art of the word' and –

> Clear and decisive proof of the fact that until now the word has been in chains is its subordination to sense.
> Until now they have maintained: 'thought dictates laws to the word and not the contrary'.
> We have pointed out this error and have provided a free language, trans-sense and universal.
> Through thought, former artists approached the word, we, however, approach it through direct comprehension.

As a climax Kruchenykh says, 'In art we announce: THE WORD BROADER THAN SENSE.' He maintains, 'Each letter, each sound is important' and says, 'Why not move away from thought and write not with words – concepts but with freely created words?' and, finally, 'We do not need intermediaries – symbols, thought, we give our own new truth and we do not serve as the reflection of some sun . . .'[35] Only by approaching the text in the spirit of the artist's decor and costumes can we hope to gain the insight which Kruchenykh and, above all, Khlebnikov in his prologue, hoped to convey. Perhaps our very partial understanding is all that was available to their contemporaries – it would seem to be the case for Livshits, who clearly appreciated the staging effects far more than the story or music.

The problem with trying to render the text in translation is the fundamental difference between modern western European languages and Russian. Perhaps by translating the opera (and other *zaum* writing) into Latin, or better still, ancient Greek, the nuances of the extension of formal grammar by the construction of unexpected parts of words and verbs could be achieved. As it is, the substitution in English or French of one word by another, or even by a group of words, cannot convey the suggestions and echoes which arise in the mind when language is distorted by *zaum* writers. The nearest English language equivalent might be James Joyce's *Finnegan's Wake* and even that ought to be listened to, read aloud by an Irishman, to gain a full experience of it.

In Act II of the opera the Elocutionist has an evocative speech, even in translation:

> how extraordinary life is without a past
> With danger but without regrets and memories . . .
> Forgotten are mistakes and failures boringly squeaking into
> one's ear you now become like a clear mirror or a rich
> reservoir where in a clear cave light-hearted goldfish
> wiggle their tails like grateful Turks. [36]

But no doubt we are not intended to understand any speech in the opera at face value. For Matyushin complained about Mayakovsky's tragedy that he

> never divorces a word from its meaning, he does not
> recognise that the sound of a word is priceless in itself. I find
> his play very important and significant, but it does not
> establish the last word or lay stones down in the quagmire
> of the future as a route for Futureland arts.

In contrast he cited 'Victory over the Sun' which, he said,

> presented the first performance on a stage in St Petersburg
> of the disintegration of concepts and words, of old staging,
> and of musical harmony.
>
> They presented a new creation, free of old conventional
> experiences and complete in itself, using seemingly
> senseless words – picture-sound – new indications of the
> future that lead into eternity and give a joyful feeling of
> strength to those who reverently will lend an ear and look
> at it. [37]

Today we shall probably turn with relief to Mayakovsky's tragedy and find that the text has more accessible meaning, the story-line carries us through. Even so, when a performance was planned in 1914 in Moscow, the artist invited to design sets found the experience profoundly moving:

> The reading produced a staggering effect on me. I ran to the
> house and began to make sketches. The city square was to
> be shown. Mayakovsky himself was to play the poet. The
> tragedy is built on a monologue. He had found in it a specific
> form which has no equal in the whole of world literature. It
> was a kind of 'utopian realism' a kind of dream of the new
> life. That is why we saw the city not only as the well-
> planned centre of population but almost as an imaginary
> setting. [38]

The artist in question was Aristarkh Lentulov, a founder member of the Knave of Diamonds; his design for Act I can be seen in colour plate 16. The description 'utopian realism' seems remarkably perceptive; even more so of Mayakovsky's approach to play writing than to Lentulov's set design.

Mayakovsky continued to write plays: 'Mystery-bouffe' in 1918 for the anniversary of the Bolshevik revolution; the 'Bed Bug' and the 'Bath House' ten years later. All three were directed by Meyerhold, the first, with settings by Malevich.

Very little is known in detail about what Malevich's sets for 'Mystery-bouffe' looked like, except that the decor was made in his geometric, non-figurative, suprematist style. The only descriptions are vague:

> a huge blue hemisphere for the world, a few cubes for the ark, geometrical backcloths.[39]

All we can surmise is that Malevich had arrived at the goal to which Livshits saw that his decor for the earlier, futurist opera was leading:

> Instead of the square and the circle to which Malevich was already attempting to reduce his painting, he was given the opportunity to operate with their volumetrical correlates, the cube and the sphere. Seizing upon them, with the mercilessness of a Savonarola, he proceeded to destroy everything which fell outside the axes which he had designated.
>
> This was a *zaum* of painting, one which anticipated the ecstatic non-objectivity of Suprematism. But how strikingly different it was from the *zaum* which the people in three-cornered hats were declaiming and singing![40]

In describing the effects achieved on the stage during the performance of 'Victory over the Sun' as anticipating Malevich's suprematist paintings, Livshits was looking back with the hindsight of familiarity to a style which was not developed until over a year later, and not exhibited for two years. An illustrated book which came out late in 1916, in which Malevich tried to explain the new style fully, was entitled, *From Cubism and Futurism to Suprematism: new painterly realism* and was illustrated with the square and the circle mentioned by Livshits [79, 80].[41]

In contrast, on the front cover of *Victory over the Sun*, of December 1913, one of Malevich's set designs for the opera is reproduced [35]. In it there remain as many representational clues as there are geometric. Clearly recognisable are the stylised edge of the sun, little aeroplane wheels, a musical note, a comma and the first two letters of Kruchenykh's name. Parts of triangles, a complete triangle, parts of circles are non-representational; the groups of parallel lines can also be read as displaced musical staves. The design shows that, at that moment, as in

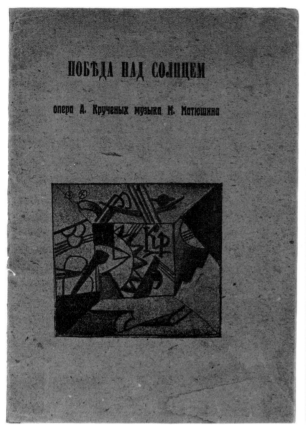

ПОБѢДА НАД СОЛНЦЕМ

опера А. Крученых музыка М. Матюшина

Ц. 60 к.

35. *Victory over the Sun*, 1913:
opera by A. Kruchenykh.
Cover with reproduction of
a set design by K. Malevich,
printed on coarse brown paper,
24 x 17 cm.

36. *Victory over the Sun*, 1913:
back cover with
drawing by David Burliuk
from *A Trap for Judges 2*
where it appears opp. p. 50
printed vertically,
with the horse the right way up

his contemporary oil painting, he was beginning not suprematism, but his cubo-futurist style (he gave that title for the first time to paintings on exhibition at the period of the production of the opera.)[42] The set design resolves the struggles between the various modern styles that he had experimented with during 1913, so well documented by his lithographs.

It was only in retrospect that Malevich understood the lasting importance of the most extreme geometric designs for the opera, most of all the black square itself, which appears as a central motif on the costume design for the Gravedigger.[43] In May 1915 when Matyushin was planning to publish 'Victory over the Sun' in a new edition, Malevich wrote to him about the black square: 'This drawing will have great significance for painting. What had been done unconsciously is now giving extraordinary results.'[44]

Even the intervening year's work which Malevich exhibited the same spring at Tramway V, showed the inspiration the opera had already provided for him. Pictures such as 'Aviator-portrait' (Russian Museum, Leningrad) and 'Englishman in Moscow' (Stedelijk Museum, Amsterdam) depend on the one hand for subject matter, and on the other for the treatment of it, on experience gained in the theatre. 'Englishman in Moscow' has sometimes been likened to a surrealist painting before its time[45] and the peculiar juxtaposition of imagery in the text of the opera itself anticipates the movement:

Д. Бурлюкъ.

37. *A Trap for Judges 2*, 1913:
drawing by David Burliuk,
printed on light blue paper,
opp. p. 46.

Let the red-rot horses
Trample
And hair will curl
Into the smell of skin! . . .[46]

Yet the way that Malevich was still composing these pictures and the others in
the same exhibition, relied on the overlapping techniques he had learned from
French cubism. In contrast, the final suprematist fruits of the opera depend
mainly on the arrangement of geometric forms adjacent to each other and
spread out on a white ground.

Strangely, the one linking factor between the books *Victory over the Sun* and
'*Vladimir Mayakovsky*' – *a Tragedy* is the participation in both of David Burliuk.
On the back of the opera was reproduced the horse and rider composition which
had been printed on the poster [36].[47] It was one of a series which was originally
used in *A Trap for Judges 2* and in some of the versions the parts of horse and rider
are so schematised that they become black geometric shapes, repeated and

spread out across the white page [37]. They seem to be analogous to the shapes which Malevich created with lights on the stage.

When *'Vladimir Mayakovsky'* – *a Tragedy* was published four months after the performance, David Burliuk provided some of the illustrations and his brother Vladimir the rest. Once again the illustrations refer back to ideas which the Burliuks had explored during the previous year, but now Vladimir in particular used freely distributed solid and outlined geometric forms arranged on the white page [38]. Admittedly, his rectangles and triangles are interspersed with the

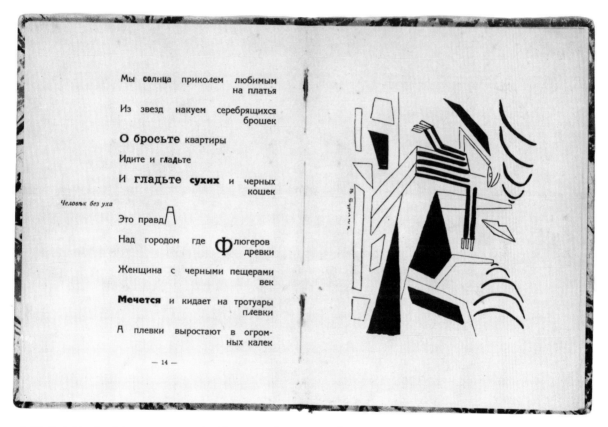

38. *'Vladimir Mayakovsky'* – *A Tragedy*, 1914: p. 14, with Vladimir Burliuk's drawing of The Man with kisses[?].

recognisable eye and trousers of Mayakovsky's character, but they are spread out on the white surface in a way very similar to Malevich's own drawings of 1914 and 1915 which lead up to his suprematist paintings.[48] This is not an influence which Malevich would ever have owned, but nonetheless it cannot be passed over.

As has been remarked elsewhere, the book itself broke new ground in graphic design and it is this connection which most obviously links the last play to be considered back to its roots in Russian futurism. *Le-Dantyu as a Beacon* is typeset

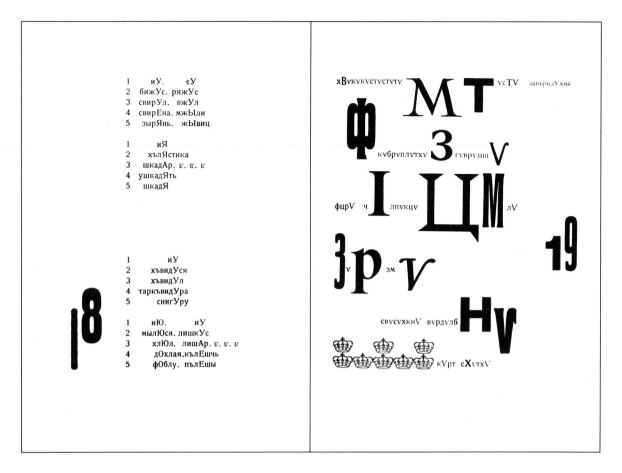

in such a visually arresting way that the content threatens to become lost on the would-be reader [31, 39].

The author, Ilya Zdanevich, published the play under the pseudonym Iliazd which he used thereafter.[49] It was one of his first works to be published in Paris where he settled as an exile. 'Le-Dantyu as a beacon' was the fifth *dra*, as Zdanevich named his dramatic works, and was the climax of a series beginning with 'Yanko the king of Albania' (*Yanko krul' albanskai*). He had written this first play in Petrograd where it was performed privately in a studio in 1916 and was not published at the time because the censor banned it. The title suggests both Marinetti's early play 'Le roi Bombance'[50] and its nineteenth-century precursor 'Ubu roi' by Alfred Jarry.[51] (The sexless frightened king, who has to be glued to his throne, sounds like a parody of the earlier heroes.)

In 1917 Zdanevich returned to his home town, Tiflis, today Tbilisi, where he wrote more plays and was able to publish 'Yanko' the following year. Kruchenykh arrived in Tiflis and joined up with his previous rival to form a new outpost of futurism, which they named 41°. Under this name Zdanevich published another play 'Easter-eyeland' (*Ostraf paskhi*) which might be seen as a forerunner of 'Le-Dantyu as a beacon'. In 'Easter-eyeland' one of the main characters was a sculptor; the play is set in 'a shop of stone coffins' and built on

39. *Le-Dantyu as a Beacon*, 1923: pp. 18–19, text and typography by Ilya Zdanevich, printed in Paris.

the theme of death and resurrection. It seems to look back to 'Victory over the Sun' where the sun had been warned:

> We will throw a dustsheet over you
> And confine you in a boarded-up concrete house![52]

Two of the main characters in 'Le-Dantyu as a beacon' are artists – painters rather than sculptors; the theme is an investigation into the relationship of reality to art. Instead of the far-away invented sculptors of 'Easter-eyeland' (related to the primitives who had made overlife-sized sculptures in the South Seas and also to the moderns who were making abstract art from squares – stone coffins) Zdanevich has chosen a 'real' painter, Mikhail Le-Dantyu, as his hero. If, as Professor Markov suggests, Zdanevich wrote the play while still in Russia, the choice of hero was even more relevant, as his friend Le-Dantyu was also a native of Tiflis and had died there in 1917.

The plot is given another dimension because, although Le-Dantyu was not a fictitious character and can therefore be seen as 'real', he is contrasted in the play with a villain, who is a 'realist' painter. The villain makes a portrait of a

40. Reproduction of 'Portrait of M. Fabbri, 1913' by M. Le-Dantyu, included in *Donkey's Tail and Target*, 1913.

dead woman, described as 'the living image of her'; Le-Dantyu paints an 'unlike' portrait of her. An example of a 'real, unlike' portrait by Mikhail Le-Dantyu can be found reproduced in *Donkey's Tail and Target* (*Oslinyi khvost i mishen*) [40]. In the play, both portraits come to life and when the unlike portrait touches the dead woman, she come to life. Then the unlike portrait kills the life-like one, setting off a series of murders, which are finally resolved by the resurrection of the forces of life. Clearly the plot functions on several levels of 'reality' especially since the language is a most advanced form of *zaum* which Markov praises as 'unbelievably inventive, expressive and funny'.[53]

Like his other *dra*, 'Le-Dantyu as a beacon' has connections with folk drama, which may have been Zdanevich's reason for choosing Le-Dantyu as his hero. Mikhail Le-Dantyu had been involved with a semi-private production of a folk play called 'King Maximillian and his unruly son Adolph' organised by the Union of Youth in St Petersburg in 1911. The performance was distinguished by an invitation to the audience to take part which was written on the poster:

> 'King Maximillian and his unruly son Adolph' 2nd part: caprices of choir with the public. People wanting to take part in the dramatic action are asked to take note of the following rules: 1. A shot from the red cannon indicates the participation of the choir after which nobody may remain in the hall except people who are masked and dressed-up (on top of their own clothes) in special loose cloaks and masks made after drawings by artists of the Union of Youth and handed out free during the interval in the artists' balcony.[54]

Le-Dantyu's participation in this kind of theatrical activity which involved the voluntary inclusion of the spectators – rather different in intention from the harassment the futurists offered an audience – lead him to formulate some theories of a new kind of drama. In 1912 he wrote notes for an article on 'Active performance' derived from his experiences both in folk theatre and futurist theatre.[55] His ideas, above all, called for a synthesis of style of the scene painter with the actors and staging so that they would together influence the spectators, not passively but actively.

As Mikhail Le-Dantyu was closely linked to Larionov's group in 1912 and 1913 it is not surprising that these theories of a rival did not have much influence on Kruchenykh and Mayakovsky in their futurist opera and tragedy, neither of which set out actively to include the audience (though both performances drew loud, negative participation – not quite what Le-Dantyu envisaged).

But Zdanevich too was in the centre of Larionov's group in those years, as biographer and spokesman and when he came to write plays he does seem to have been strongly influenced by Le-Dantyu's ideas, drawing on the lively traditions of folk drama as well as developing futurist language. He knew Le-Dantyu well: he and his brother shared a memorable journey in the country around Tiflis with Mikhail Le-Dantyu, looking for the Georgian painter, Niko Pirosmanashvili. (The Soviet film, 'Pirosmani' reconstructs it with great beauty.)

When Zdanevich chose to commemorate Le-Dantyu in the title role of his last *dra*, he was drawing together a wide spectrum of ideas. In the final publication of the book he outstripped most western European typographical invention while anticipating surrealism by continuing the Russian futurist tradition which he and Kruchenykh had pushed further in Tiflis. Beyond the reach of the censor they had developed the double meanings of words to a degree of obscenity which was unthinkable earlier. Even the experiments with print had been pioneered in 1914 in Russia in *'Vladimir Mayakovsky' – a Tragedy* [12]. Yet, with all its rich dimensions of meaning and invention, *Le-Dantyu as a beacon* has finally to be seen as an epitaph rather than as a beacon itself. Already in 1923 in Berlin, El Lissitzky printed the poems by Mayakovsky entitled *For the voice* (*Dlya golosa*)[56] in a way that showed that quite a new order could be established in typographical experiment. Likewise, in the realm of theatre itself, Meyerhold was beginning new relationships with his audience, using the scene design, acting and staging to involve the spectators. Popova's multi-media design for Meyerhold's production of 'The Earth in Turmoil' fulfilled in Moscow all the ideas which Le-Dantyu had noted in 1912.[57] In Russia the development out of futurism was not dada or surrealism, but constructivism. That, however, is beyond the reaches of this study.

41. *Worldbackwards*, 1912: leaf 1,
poem by A. Kruchenykh,
drawing by M. Larionov,
lithographed by V. Titaev.

4

GRAPHIC DESIGN

It would be hard to find a group of books which could rival those published by Russian futurists in the inventiveness of graphic design [colour plate 1]. Although the main flow of activity lasted not much more than eighteen months – from October 1912, when the first books were registered, new books continued to appear sporadically and there were resurgences of activity leading finally to the constructivist books of the early 1920s. These are generally better known in the West, as many were printed in Germany. Constructivist books were designed by a new generation of artists for many of the authors of futurist books, especially Mayakovsky and Kruchenykh. Early in 1914, futurist graphic design already presaged features more commonly identified with constructivist books.

All the books share the characteristic that they were produced by artists, for the majority of Russian futurist poets having trained at art school, crossed from drawing to writing, from art to literature. There arose what is still today an avant-garde idea, that the artist could express creative ideas using words instead of, or as well as, marks. The technique chosen for printing the first books emphasised the fundamental unity of the two kinds of activity: handwriting was intended to convey the personality of the poet in the same way that his drawing reveals the identity of the artist [41]. Writing and drawing were reproduced by lithography – not the mechanical photolithography used today, but a hand-process by which the professional artist at the printers transferred the work and printed it.

It was not a new idea for artists to be involved in publishing, but previously they had more often been concerned specifically with making book illustrations or helping to produce magazines about art, than in making illustrated, hand-written books of new poetry. An exception was William Blake, whose early nineteenth-century illustrated, hand-made but printed poetry books can be seen as a prototype for Kruchenykh's first books.[1] However, Blake had to invent his own engraving technique to transfer his handwriting in order for it to be readable (for direct engraving prints the image in reverse).

The development of lithography and, more especially, lithographic transfer processes, gave more freedom to an artist who wished to convey complete unity to the page, for it was a process which allowed the hand-written text and accompanying image to be reproduced quickly and at a low cost.

In Russia, many of the generation of World of Art artists, of whom Bilibin was the most prolific in the field, had made very beautiful illustrated children's books at the turn of the century. These were traditional Russian myths and legends presented with colourful borders to the pages and striking pictures, often on the same page as the text. The method of printing was chromo-lithography, using subtle, dark tones, which gave the originals a density of colouring which cannot be appreciated in the otherwise very faithful modern reprints published over the last few years in Soviet Russia.[2]

Some of the same illustrations and related subjects were printed as postcards in a series which bears a distinguishing device with a central red cross and the words 'in aid of the community of St Evgeniya'. The quality of printing, like the quality of the children's books, is very high. Many of the postcards bear the name of the artist and 'lit. N Kadushina', or, more often, 'lit. D Ilina', indicating the name of the lithographer, and an interesting account of the role of such a professional, working in London from 1896, is given by Thomas Griffits in his book, *The Rudiments of Lithography*.[3] The early chapters describe the complexity of the work of the lithographic artist employed by a printer and show how his contribution to the finished result was so great that he certainly deserved recognition by the inclusion of his name on the lithograph together with that of the artist, in the same way that an engraver was credited on a print. Especially in the case of colour work, the appearance of the finished illustration or postcard would depend entirely on his skill, for the process was quite different to mechanical photographic reproductive methods to be found on contemporary postcards made as reproductions of art works.

World of Art artists who made lithographed postcards, were, of course, involved in the art magazine from which they took their name. *The World of Art* (*Mir iskusstva*) 1898–1904 was only the first of a large number of lavish journals to succeed one another in Russia, where there was greater publishing activity in the field of art than in any other European country. It was followed by *The Scales* (*Vesy*) 1904–9, *The Golden Fleece* (*Zolotoe runo*) 1906–9 (1910) and *Apollon* 1909–17. These informative journals, combining new literature and reproductions of art with art criticism, relying on artists to design elaborate covers, signal the enlightened milieu in which new art movements arose.

For example, *The Golden Fleece* was published by a rich patron, who was himself an amateur artist, Nikolai Ryabushinsky.[4] He was responsible for financing avant-garde exhibitions, he bought avant-garde work and some of the pictures were reproduced in his journal. So, when the new journal, *Impressionists' Studio* (*Studiya impressionistov*) was published in February 1910, it must at first have appeared as a St Petersburg successor to *The Golden Fleece*, especially as the editor had organised an 'Impressionist' exhibition the previous year.

The editor was Dr Nikolai Kulbin, a man of altogether more modest means than his predecessors in the field, but the single number of *Impressionists' Studio* matched most previous books with its fine quality printing, including colour reproductions [colour plates 14 and 15]. Only in content were new ideas presented, in format it could easily be confused with symbolist journals.

The graphic design of the contemporary *A Trap for Judges* (*Sadok sudei*) also looks rather symbolist today, but it is unusual in being printed entirely on the reverse side of patterned wallpaper [42], with the title label glued to the

42. *A Trap for Judges*, 1910: double opening to show patterned wallpaper and a portrait of Elena Guro, one of the contributors, by Vladimir Burliuk.

wallpaper cover [colour plate 1b]. As the first collection of avant-garde poetry, written largely by artists and presented under a deliberately provocative title, it established what proved to be a most important precedent, although it did not form a pattern for Russian avant-garde publications. In 1913, after a second anthology was published with the same title, Kruchenykh drew attention to the first *A Trap for Judges* giving a revised, falsified, publication date – 1908 so as to appear to pre-empt the foundation manifesto of Italian futurism. [5] So, three years later, the avant-garde looked back and saw in this book the first eruption of a new approach to the book.

Kruchenykh's first three books, of autumn 1912, broke entirely new ground in commercial book production. *Old-time love* (*Starinnaya lyubov*) [1, 2, 43] is about the size of a postcard, with the folded pages printed on one side and stapled together. The drawings which decorate the pages complement the handwriting of the poems but the style used by Larionov is futurist – the full-size drawings [57] on two pages are so overlaid with 'lines of force', rays, or, to the uninitiated, scribbles, that the hand-made look was clearly intended, not to rival the fastidious elegance of symbolist publications, but in deliberate antithesis. The same is true of *A Game in Hell* (*Igra v adu*) [5–8] and *Worldbackwards*

(*Mirskontsa*), but the style was different, closer to an updating of the traditional popular Russian broadsheet or *lubok*.

Because of his training as a graphic artist, Kruchenykh must be credited with the design of the books. The originality of his approach can be measured by comparing the appearance of those which he initiated, right up to the 1920s, with those to which he was only a contributor, or which were published independently. Those directly under his supervision surpass in design those of nearly all his contemporaries, his only rival being the poet Vasily Kamensky, who produced two outstandingly original books early in 1914.[6]

In each case, Kruchenykh seems to have been able to build up an extremely productive relationship with an artist/collaborator. In the first four months he was certainly aided by the close collaboration of Larionov and Goncharova, who provided art work in the spirit of the poetry written by himself and Khlebnikov, the co-author of two of the books. Kruchenykh's previous experience with the two artists was in their contributions to a series of postcards which he published in 1912, which perhaps gave him the idea of turning to this original approach to illustrated book production.

Kruchenykh's postcards were printed in black and white and showed artists' drawings in various styles. They may have been in emulation of those made by World of Art artists or, possibly, of slightly later European examples. Avant-garde artists' postcards had been published by the Wiener Werkstätte and a set by Oskar Kokoschka, made in about 1908, in colour lithography, is likely to have been known in Russia.[7] In Munich in 1910, Franz Marc prepared a set which did not get further than the printer's proof stage, but which may well have been known by Goncharova and Larionov who were in correspondence with Kandinsky.[8]

As postcards, Kruchenykh published sets of twelve drawings by each artist; Mikhail Larionov's brother Ivan contributed as well as Goncharova and Larionov themselves. On the reverse was printed the artist's name, the title of his drawing, 'published by A Kruchenykh' and the name of the firm of printers, 'tip-lit V Rikhter, Moscow.'[9] The same inscription, typeset in the same manner, can be read on the back cover of the first of Kruchenykh's books to be published, *Old-time love* [43] and *A Game in Hell*. The typesetting on the same cover with the otherwise entirely hand-drawn text and images seems out of place and on subsequent books the information was added in handwriting [41, 45]. But it was also different: an abbreviation of the word lithographed alone was included, making clear the way in which the books were printed.

The kind of lithography used in Kruchenykh's books, was a hand-process, distinguished by the general designation 'autolithography'. The degree of participation by the artist who originated the image or the handwriting would vary. The printing was done by the professional, rather than the artist himself,

43. *Old-time Love*, 1912:
back cover design by M. Larionov,
showing vase of flowers and
two butterflies as front cover [1]
but with vase tipped over;
printer's inscription,
bottom right hand corner.

from a lithographic stone, or sometimes, a zinc plate. The artist rarely worked on the stone, but provided the drawing and writing on paper. Special transfer papers were available, ready prepared for an artist to draw on, either with a lithographic crayon or pen, though cartridge paper could also be used.

Larionov and Goncharova seem to have enjoyed exploring the technical possibilities of lithography, which they exploited in an original way, playing with texture and line in varying ways in the six different books on which they worked with Kruchenykh. They adapted for lithography ideas which they took from many sources. For example, Larionov seems to have been influenced by the title pages and portraits which Kokoschka made for the Berlin art magazine *Der Sturm* between 1910 and 1912, his calligraphic style remarkably anticipating Larionov's rayism, as well as being very much suited to use with handwriting.[10]

However, the inspiration behind much of Larionov and Goncharova's graphic experiments is to be found in their interest in all forms of prints, demonstrated in a huge exhibition which they mounted in April 1913. The catalogue proves that many of the exhibits belonged personally to Larionov.[11] He had amassed a varied collection of graphics, including French *images d'épinal*, Japanese woodcuts, Persian manuscripts, Chinese and Indian material, as well as examples of the Russian *lubok*.

Not surprisingly, the *lubok* was a favourite source of inspiration to Larionov and Goncharova as well as to other avant-garde artists. The traditional broadsheet was originally introduced into Russia from Germany and probably acquired the name *lubok* from the limewood block from which it was printed, though during the seventeenth century a technique of copper engraving was used as well. The *lubok* of the seventeenth and eighteenth century is the most original: folklore heroes, calendars, zodiacs are reproduced, as well as parodies of state occasions with animals replacing humans. The pictures are usually hand-coloured and images are printed on the same sheet as the text, arranged next to, or sometimes below, a sequence of small pictures like a page from a modern comic book. The type used is an old face, irregularly printed, so that the *lubok* has some of the quality of a hand-made object.[12]

Larionov and Goncharova borrowed very directly from *lubok* imagery, although they only occasionally used the amazing abstract patterns which traditional designers employed as shading on the images. One rare example of this practice is on a cat, drawn by Larionov, shown lying next to a nude, published first as 'Katapska Venus' in Zdanevich's biography of the artist and then in the Italian futurist journal, *Lacerba*, as 'The Soldier's Venus'.[13]

As book followed book in the autumn and winter of 1912–13 the originality of graphic invention seemed unending. *Worldbackwards* went on sale in December, a miscellany of poetry and drawings, enclosed in an ambitious paper cover on to which was glued an original collage by Goncharova [colour plate 2]. Each copy has a variation in the shape of the cut-out leaf design: some are cut in green or black shiny paper, others in gold-embossed paper, so that each type is individually distinguished from others. The book includes pages of rubber-stamped words, sometimes announcing who the next section is written by, or arranged with the words forming a short poem [colour plate 3]. These groups of words look as though they were set up on a child's printing outfit, with coloured letters added in afterwards, using a rough stencil or potato-cut.

Words are given freedom in stylised disorder before the Italian futurists had achieved their 'words in freedom' (*parole in libertà*). In *Worldbackwards*, a long poem by Kruchenykh is printed without capital letters or punctuation, exactly contemporary with the French poem 'Zone' by Apollinaire.[14] Kruchenykh's title, 'Journey across the whole world' probably gave another French poet, Blaise Cendrars, the idea for his *La Prose du Transsibérien* on which he began work early in 1913. When this poem was finally printed and decorated by Sonia Delaunay, who was herself a Russian, it was to be one of the very few western

European equivalents to the Russian futurist books; it was first exhibited in autumn 1913.[15]

In design and inventiveness, *Worldbackwards* can be seen as a rival to the earlier, Munich almanac, edited by Kandinsky and Franz Marc, which had appeared in May 1912. Through the Russian contributors, David Burliuk and Goncharova, *Der Blaue Reiter* must have been known to Kruchenykh, who, however, in no way imitated it. Where Kandinsky had provided reproductions of Russian folk art, Larionov and his friends drew their own; where the almanac contained writing about art and literature and music, *Worldbackwards* consisted of the newest trends in art and literature presented without comment. A limited number of copies of *Der Blaue Reiter* included original artists' prints as well as the reproductions of art works; *Worldbackwards* consisted entirely of lithographed or rubber-stamped pages. Whereas the Munich book gave the appearance of a well-produced, relatively ordinary book, (in spite of Kandinsky's determination to make it altogether different and original, 'an artists' book'), the Moscow book has a hand-made quality stemming in part from the collage glued on to the cover. It disrupts all expectations: pieces of tracing paper are tipped in, neatly protecting the most antagonising lithographs, with 'drawing by Nataliya Goncharova' rubber-stamped on the corner to identify the lithograph underneath; a drawing by Vladimir Tatlin [44] reveals his brief interest in a calligraphic style in which he plays with the possibilities of the medium of a lithographic pen.[16]

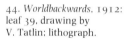

44. *Worldbackwards*, 1912: leaf 39, drawing by V. Tatlin; lithograph.

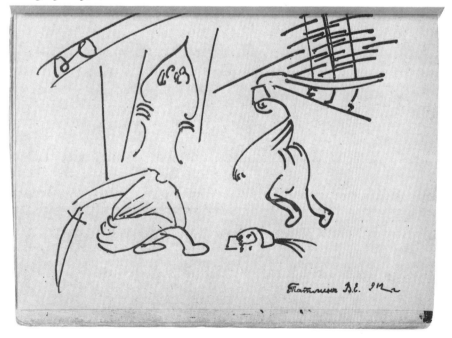

45. *A Selection of Poems 1907–14*, by V. Khlebnikov: final leaf of 16 illustrations by Pavel Filonov, printed by Svet.

Like most of the other artists, Tatlin signed his drawing. Goncharova often used only a monogram [6, 7], while Larionov usually signed his name in full. On two pages in *Worldbackwards*, Larionov's signature appears on the right at the bottom of the page and the name of the professional lithographer, V. Titaev, is placed on the other side of the image [3, 41]. More usually, the name of the lithographer is written at the back of each book: Rikhter, Mukharsky, Titaev in Moscow and Svet in St Petersburg, sometimes identified simply by their address [45].

The lithographic technique has often been discussed in a rather superficial way. As early as February 1913, in *A Trap for Judges 2* (*Sadok sudei 2*), one of the points in the manifesto, signed among others by Kruchenykh, reads:

> 5c Therefore in Moscow we have published books (of autographs) [which are] 'self-written'.

By this very unclear description, Kruchenykh seems to be insisting on the importance of the hand of the writer and artist. Those who have interpreted this statement and the evidence of the books to mean that the artist and writer worked directly on the stone, either forget the impracticability of writing the long texts backwards, or assume that the technique was modern offset lithography whereby the marks on the stone are taken up on to a roller in negative form and then printed positively.

However, by using transfer paper, both artist and writer can give positive images to the printer exactly as they will appear in the finished book. Another advantage of working on transfer papers is that the work does not need to be done at the printers, but can be done by the artist and writer when and where he finds it convenient, and the finished result is not inferior to work drawn directly on the stone.

In the case of Russian futurist books it seems that illustration and handwriting were not always prepared together, but were lined up by the professional doing the transferring, for a number of loose copies of Larionov and Goncharova's lithographs exist separate from the written page.[17] (Two of Goncharova's devils, drawn for the edge of a page of writing in *A Game in Hell*, were printed finally side by side [7].) Although the lithographs are not, of course, individually numbered, the *tirages* of the books were small and some were printed in numbered editions. At first it was the deliberate intention of the avant-garde not to make conventionally valuable or beautiful books. The details of printing have only become important since the books and, regrettably, lithographs detached from them have recently acquired considerable commercial value. Unfortunately, this value is not even the same as that of French *éditions de luxe*, where it lies in the whole book, but is that of an artist's original print, which is far from the earliest spirit of the enterprise.

But notwithstanding the original, almost dadaist, conception of the books devised by Kruchenykh, soon after Larionov and Goncharova stopped collaborating with him, they each turned the experience they had gained in a new medium to their own advantage. Goncharova made coloured lithographs for an *édition de luxe* for Sergei Bobrov, a writer, who, though much less radical in his approach than Kruchenykh, was interested in modern book design. The conventionally printed book of his poems, entitled *Gardeners over the vines* (*Vertogradari nad lozami*), had the format of a modern paperback, but this external appearance is deceptive, for, between ten gatherings are double-page blue and brown lithographs [colour plates 6 and 7]. These were the earliest examples of lithographs made by the artist on the stone and Goncharova seems to have been the only futurist artist to do this in Russia. The edition was slightly larger than Kruchenykh's early books, some of which sold out quite quickly, and the copies are numbered.

The last section of *Gardeners over the vines* was devoted to a short article by Bobrov on the originality of Goncharova's illustrations.[18] The publication date almost coincided with *Donkey's Tail and Target* (*Oslinyi khvost i mishen*), as both books were registered in *Knizhnaya letopis* in the second half of July. In an article which gave *Donkey's Tail and Target* its title, Varsanovy Parkin described the characteristics of artists' work shown in both exhibitions.[19] Throughout the article, single examples of lithographs by Larionov from Kruchenykh's books were individually pasted on to gaps on the pages as illustrations, with the title printed beside each. Interestingly, the author ended with the inscription 'Paris' – so that one can deduce that copies of Kruchenykh's books reached France quite soon after they went on sale in Russia. (They were, of course, an admirable size for posting.)

A year later, when Larionov and Goncharova held an exhibition at the Galerie Paul Guillaume in Paris, they each included lithographs from the books among their paintings. So already, in 1914, they saw their lithographs as independent art works, even in cases where they had originally made the drawing as a definite illustration to a specific poem.

The lithographs which Malevich made for Kruchenykh's books would also appear to be ideal for exhibiting, so it is surprising that there is no evidence that they were ever shown separately. However, at some later date, he apparently gave the Swiss artist Hans Arp copies of both lithographs for *Explodity* (*Vzorval*), (now in the collection of the print room at the Kunstmuseum, Basel).[20] Each is very slightly larger in height and width than those tipped into the book [67, 69] and Malevich has added water-colour, so it is possible that he had intended at some time to exhibit them.

In fact, the lithographs by Malevich look rather out of place in *Explodity*. They look strangely formal, for instead of the random scattering, typical of most of the pages [11], his imagery, though hard to read, clearly has its own formal logic. His title, 'Simultaneous death of a man in an aeroplane and at the railway' is the most careful piece of handwriting in the book [67]. On other pages, words are spilled across the sheet, closely linked with images drawn by Kulbin [71]; the book has a more heterogeneous look than the previous miscellany, *Worldbackwards*, where only a few pages had rubber-stamped poems [colour plate 3]. In the later, second edition of *Explodity* [colour plate 1d], the same rubber-stamped poems were replaced by hand-written versions with decoration by Rozanova [46, 47]. Other pages were the kind of double-ruled paper which children used to be given in exercise books, designed to improve the neatness of their writing; here the rubber-stamping is scattered about the page in deliberate untidiness.

However dissimilar the pages in *Explodity*, they shared the same size. The same cannot be said of other books which Kruchenykh published after he moved to St Petersburg. For example, in the conventionally printed *Let's Grumble*

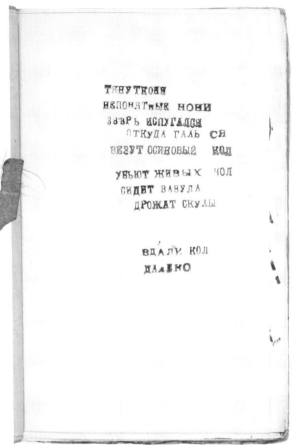
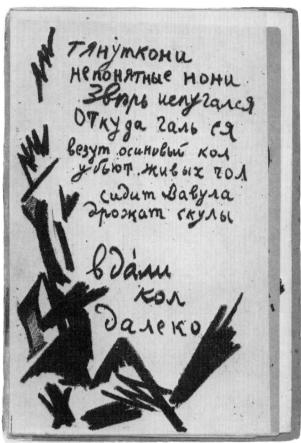

46, 47. *Explodity,*
editions 1, 1913 and 2, 1914:
the same poem
by A. Kruchenykh,
rubber-stamped in first edition;
hand-written and
lithographed with decoration
by O. Rozanova in second.

(*Vozropshchem*) [colour plate 21], lithographs by Malevich and Rozanova were tipped-in inside the front cover, where they clash with the format [48, 49]. The size of all the lithographs made in 1913 by Malevich and Rozanova is more uniform than the books.

A number of their lithographs were printed on greenish paper and the drawings were evidently transferred, several together, to a single stone. From this, sheets were printed which were then cut and used in the different books. Proof is given by the slightly inaccurate cutting which has resulted in the edge of an image by Rozanova being just visible along the left-hand side of Malevich's 'Peasant woman' glued to the front cover of the copy of *Piglets* (*Porosyata*) in the British Library collection [colour plate 19]. This can be seen in the original even though the book has been bound in a hard cover, so that less of the lithograph is visible than usual. There is no lithograph by Rozanova in *Piglets*, which, together with the dates that the books went on sale, suggests that Malevich and Rozanova's lithographs may have been printed on only a few occasions. *Explodity* and *Let's Grumble* were registered a week apart in June, so the lithographs may have been printed together and distributed between the books.

However, this is not the case with the lithographs printed on greenish paper. The books in which they were used were registered in mid-August and mid-

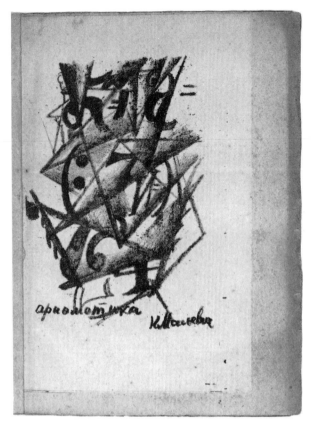

October, but Malevich's figure of a reaper on the lithograph glued to the cover of *The Word as Such* (*Slovo kak takovoe*) [colour plate 22] does not appear stylistically to belong after the photographic reproductions of drawings, which included a reaper [77], used in *The Three* (*Troe*), published in mid-September. Malevich planned the lithograph cover for *The Three* in July, for there is a photograph taken then of Kruchenykh holding up the drawing in the company of Malevich and Matyushin.[21] Although the same format, the drawing is not identical with the design finally printed [50], so it does not prove when the one used was drawn. Furthermore, because the central figure and the comma below it are depicted the wrong way round, it could be argued that Malevich intended to use transfer lithography for the wording and proposed to work directly on the stone for the figure and comma. For practical reasons, this seems unlikely: Matyushin, who published *The Three*, lived in St Petersburg and Malevich was still living in Moscow. Although it was natural for Malevich to make the drawings on transfer paper either in Moscow, just before he left for St Petersburg, or, more likely, when he arrived on his occasional visits to the capital, these were infrequent enough for him to have provided a number of transfer drawings each time. Judging by the experience of other print makers, it takes so long to make direct lithographs on the stone that Malevich would scarcely have had time.

48, 49. *Let's Grumble*, 1913: 'Arithmetic' by K. Malevich; first lithograph on white paper, tipped-in before text, 17.5 x 11 cm.
Head by O. Rozanova; third lithograph on white paper, tipped-in before text, 17.4 x 11 cm.

50. *The Three*, 1913:
poems and text
by A. Kruchenykh,
V. Khlebnikov and E. Guro.
Lithographed cover design
by K. Malevich,
in memory of E. Guro,
20 x 20 cm.

The Soviet historian, Nikolai Khardzhiev, has recently published some information which throws doubt on Malevich having any experience in the printer's shop. He disclosed the fact that in 1919 'the drawings by Malevich for the album *Suprematism* [*34 drawings*] were lithographed by El Lissitzky'.[22] Had Kruchenykh not always used a professional, Malevich would no doubt have had the experience to lithograph his own drawings. But when he went to teach at the art school in Vitebsk this was not the case: Khardzhiev not only assures us that 'the polygraphic master of the Vitebsk art school was the printer of 1000 numbered copies of '*On New Systems in Art*', but that El Lissitzky was also responsible for the design on the cover of that book, although Malevich was the author of the lithographs glued inside [81].[23]

So far, only the graphic design of Kruchenykh (and for *The Three*, perhaps of Malevich) has been discussed. A different approach is apparent in the books for which David Burliuk was responsible. His first book, *A Slap in the Face of Public Taste* (*Poshchechina obshchestvennomu vkusu*), was conventionally printed but distinguished by its sackcloth cover with the aggressive title printed on it in purple lettering [colour plate 1e]. The choice may have been influenced by Kruchenykh, but Burliuk's next book reflects his personal taste. It was called *Service Book of the Three* (*Trebnik troikh*) and went on sale in the first week of April

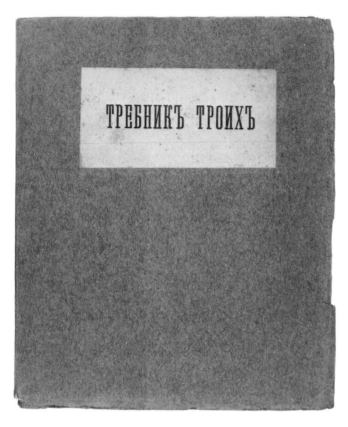

ТРЕБНИКЪ ТРОИХЪ

51. *The Service-book of the Three*, 1913:
poems by V. Mayakovsky, V. Khlebnikov and D. & N. Burliuk (the latter written as 'D.N.' to preserve the idea of 'three' in the title). Cover of grey wrapping paper with printed label pasted on, 21 x 17.6 cm.

1913 [51]. Conventionally printed poems by Khlebnikov, Mayakovsky and the Burliuk brothers were interspersed with drawings by Mayakovsky, Tatlin and the Burliuks [65, 66]. Its more orthodox appearance reflects the taste of Burliuk rather than his collaborators, for, in June, the same publishers brought out a book of Mayakovsky's poems, in a quite different style. Mayakovsky's handwritten lithographed book, *I (Ya)*, has wrappers designed by himself and illustrations by fellow art students, Vasily Chekrygin and Lev Zhegin.[24] It looks like one of Kruchenykh's 'hand-made' books, but lacks the technical brilliance of the books he had produced with Larionov and Goncharova.

David Burliuk made no entirely lithographed books at this time. Those for which he was responsible later in 1913 are conventionally printed by printers in south Russia, according to his own recollections. They include coloured illustrations and are the first books to have the word *futuristy* printed on the covers. The techniques for the colour illustrations by the Burliuks (David and Vladimir are jointly credited) are interesting.

The first of these books to go on sale was called *The Bung* (*Zatychka*) and came out at the end of October. The illustrations by Vladimir Burliuk were made on one large sheet of white paper, cut across and the two double-page lithographs thus formed were stapled in between the gatherings. One of them is remarkable for the hand-applied colour (red, blue and green) crudely washed across the images [colour plate 11]. The intention was no doubt to give separation of colour and line so that each has independent validity, as a parallel to the poem 'Heights' (*Vysoty*) by Kruchenykh, consisting only of vowels, which was printed in their next book. It was not the first time a book had been hand-coloured, as twenty-five copies of *Pomade* (*Pomada*) had been painted by Larionov. Also, at this time, Rozanova was colouring one hundred copies of *A Duck's Nest of Bad Words* (*Utinoe gnezdyshko . . . durnykh slov*).[25] But if the whole edition of *The Bung* was coloured, even as crudely as this, the work involved in colouring four hundred and fifty copies must have been considerable.

The next Burliuk book was *The Croaked Moon* (*Dokhlaya luna*). It contained two prints which are described on the cover as etchings. Each is made with a single colour [colour plate 10], but each copy of the first edition seems to include two different prints, which have the appearance of being artist's originals. However, the subjects on the whole are rather barbaric, so they are also typically futurist, a turning upside-down of the idea of an *édition de luxe* together with the literal use of images the wrong way up. *The Croaked Moon* has the date 'Autumn 1913' printed on the cover [colour plate 1c], but was not registered in *Knizhnaya letopis* until the first week of 1914 – when the printing date was confirmed as 1913. A second edition, with changes, bears 'Spring 1914' on the cover.

A third book published by David Burliuk had a further variation in technique: the conventionally printed text of *The Milk of Mares* (*Moloko kobylits*) included not only lithographs, but two photographic reproductions and two, apparently hand-made, drawings [colour plate 9]. These are roughly made with coloured brush-strokes on a single piece of cartridge paper, bound round one gathering. Smudges of paint occur on the reverse of one of the drawings in the British Library copy which indicate original work, though, with an edition of four hundred copies, the labour involved seems unbelievable. (There is no indication given in either this book, or *The Bung*, that only some copies had coloured illustrations.) The photographic reproductions included in *The Milk of Mares* were of paintings by Aleksandra Ekster, possibly paid for by this wealthy artist. Her work was also reproduced in the *First Journal of Russian Futurists 1–2* (*Pervyi zhurnal russkikh futuristov 1–2*) which came out a few weeks later, before 20 March.

In this single number of the *First Journal* (the only issue to appear) two of David and Vladimir Burliuk's lithographs were printed rather crudely in a three colour process (red, yellow and black). As can be seen in colour plate 8, which is a close-up of a small drawing printed on the rather large page, the colour registration is poor. However, the prints give the journal the appearance of having been designed to rival European publications; it is typical of a new phase in graphic design which dates from Marinetti's visit to Russia.

On his visit early in 1914, Marinetti was shown *Te li le* which went on sale a few weeks later. It marked a remarkable achievement in technique, but almost

no advance in design. Fifty copies were made by hectography, which is a
gelatine duplicating process, like the old jellygraphs used by amateurs for
reproducing a small number of copies. The advantage of the process is that
colour can be used and *Te li le* was printed in numbered copies using pink,
yellow, blue, mauve and gold [colour plates 1f, 12, 13]. All the colours sink into
the paper to give unsurpassed unity to the pages. Kruchenykh reprinted his
zaum poem which here begins '*dyr bul shchyl*' in splendid coloured writing: the
ornament round it balancing the *zaum* words. It was Kruchenykh's favourite
poem which he had first included in *Pomade* and used again in *The Word as such*,
though, curiously, each version differs slightly from the others.[26]

Yet, in spite of Marinetti's admission that nothing like *Te li le* had been
published in western Europe, the book sums up the achievements of the previous
year, rather than breaking new ground. The same is true of a second edition of *A
Game in Hell* which was a revised version of the original, newly hand-written

52. *A Game in Hell*, 1914:
second, augmented edition
of hand-written poem by
A. Kruchenykh and V. Khlebnikov.
Lithographed cover design
by K. Malevich, 19 x 14 cm.

and with lithographs by Rozanova and Malevich [52]. It looked, early in 1914, as though Kruchenykh's originality was drying up.

A challenge came from the fruitful partnership of David Burliuk with Vasily Kamensky. At the end of February a book went on sale with poems printed on the reverse side of a colourful wallpaper, decorated with bold zoo animals and entitled *The Naked One among the Clad* (*Nagoi sredi odetykh*). It was illustrated by A. Kravtsov, an amateur artist whom Kamensky, Burliuk and Mayakovsky had met on their futurist tour, who was credited as joint author of the book; his drawings are weak for an otherwise remarkable book. The same poems were printed on another striking wallpaper, with large images of flowers, under the title *Tango with Cows* (*Tango s korovami*), with lithographs by David and Vladimir Burliuk which fit the pages in a way parallel to the poems. Both books are similar in format, the top right-hand corner of the square being cut off to form a five-sided figure. Kamensky's poems are devised with words printed in varying typefaces, arranged in ways appropriate to each poem. One example is made of columns of letters narrowing into a pyramid shape, which is sculptural in its effect; on other pages words are fitted into compartments created by lines within a square, dividing the page space.

So visual are Kamensky's poems, that they were shown in the No 4 art exhibition later in the spring [55]. The catalogue heading is 'ferro-concrete poetry', a term often now abbreviated and used as 'concrete poetry', signifying modern avant-garde poems with an unusual layout. The fuller term, invented by Kamensky for poems, implies the (then new) technology of reinforced concrete – pouring concrete into a prepared mould in which rods have been laid to give structural strength. If the five-sided page is seen as the mould, the lines dividing it up can be interpreted as rods giving the poem strength. Since the Russian futurists had been criticising Marinetti for the onomatopaeic character of his poetry, it is fitting that in his new writing Kamensky began to explore words in a new kind of framework. He appears to have chosen the term 'ferro-concrete' to describe the arrangement of words on the page in direct contrast to the Italian futurists' 'words in freedom.'[27]

As Kamensky belonged to a rival group, it is surprising that his poems were included in the No 4 exhibition, which was arranged in Moscow in April by Larionov. Kamensky was one of only two artists other than those of Larionov's immediate group to take part. Perhaps it was because of a slight connection between Kamensky's poems and examples of rayist poetry [54] which had been printed in *Donkey's Tail and Target* the previous year. These had been included as the literary equivalent of Larionov's rayist style of painting and contrasted with an example of an Italian futurist poem, by Aldo Palazzeschi [53]. The Italian poem is reproduced in Cyrillic letters and reveals an almost exclusively onomatopaeic approach, visually very repetitive.

A direct line can be drawn from the rayist poetry [54], through Kamensky's page poems [55], to Apollinaire's experiments with visual poetry. The French poet called his experiments *calligrammes*; he arranged letters and words to form a picture of the subject. As they were first printed in the June and July/August numbers of *Les Soirées de Paris*, they were antedated by the Russian experiments.[28]

Of the books published in the spring of 1914, *'Vladimir Mayakovsky' – a Tragedy* proved finally the most influential as graphic design [12]. The text of

55 (opposite). *First Journal of Russian Futurists 1–2*, 1914: p. 25, V. Kamensky, 'Ferro-concrete poem' dedicated to David Burliuk.

Фру Фру Фру
Уги Уги Уги
Игу Игу Игу
Ага Ага Ага
Поэт забавляется
Безумно
Безмѣрно
А а а а а
Е е е е е
И и и и и
О о о о о
У у у у у
А Е И О У

53. *Donkey's Tail and Target*, 1913: p. 138, detail showing a poem by the Italian futurist, A. Palazzeschi.

54. *Donkey's Tail and Target*, 1913: p. 146, showing examples of rayist poetry by A. Semenov.

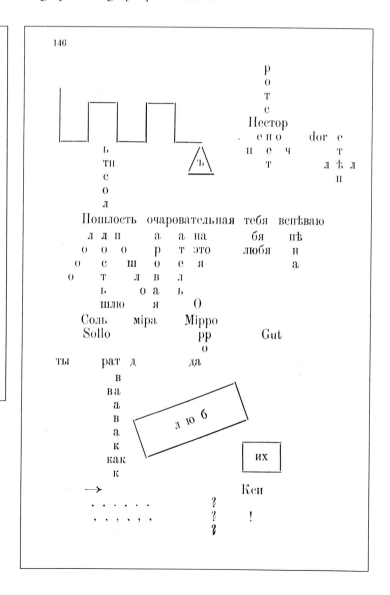

ЖЕЛЕЗОБЕТОННАЯ ПОЭМА

Д. Бурлюку.

СКЕТинг

РЖ

Льются
ЛИКИ
КЛИКИ
РОЛИКИ
кролики
КОРОЛИКИ
Журчей
ЖУРЧАНІЙ
СТОЛИЦІ
СНЕГ
ЛИ
і

Д
МЫ
УМЫ
ДУМЫ

ВЕТЕР
БоА
ФЛАГИ

ВАЛЬС т-та-та-

Е

ДвИжЕнІя

КтО гвоздика
Н а НаРцИсС
? РОЗА

ноги
ноги
А
ПОДСКОКИ

ФРЭК

ФРАК

перчатки

ТалстуХ

ТАНгО

ПЬЕРО

стенах

кто?
дѣвочка
СКОКИ
КОКИ
ко
КоТкА
хлябь челюстей
СУТЕНЕР

Ноги

ДЖЕНТЛЬМЕНЫ

РАДЖА
ОТТОМАН
англійскій
проборъ
Инструкторара

ЭЛекТР

ПиРоСы

лько

АФЕРМ

тЕ № $6^6 6_6 6^6 6_6 6$

Mayakovsky's play is printed in a strong typeface in short lines, staggered down the page. Capital letters and bold type are introduced unexpectedly to give greater emphasis and provide visual texture on the pages. It was designed by Vladimir and David Burliuk whose drawings are printed on pages opposite, making a visual parallel rather than precisely illustrating the tragedy [33, 38]. Since Mayakovsky's poetry provided such a challenge to book designers after the Revolution, it is not surprising that Rodchenko and El Lissitzky should have looked back, ignoring the conventionally printed reprint of the tragedy of 1916, to the original, telling, 1914 edition which provided a direct inspiration for what became a new, constructive approach to graphic design. For in the early 1920s, anyone looking back at the books of the heyday of futurist graphic design, would have seen it as one of the very few books to inspire a new approach. El Lissitzky went so far as to credit an English book with having shown a new example of typography, namely the vorticists' *Blast*; perhaps even he overlooked this Russian prototype.[29]

In retrospect, the early hand-written, lithographed futurist books must have taken on the guise of art works, or have been too recently connected with the acute shortages of the civil war years. Kruchenykh had made several lithographed books in Tiflis such as *Learn Art* (*Uchites khudogi*) [30], and Malevich had made two in Vitebsk. What was wanted for a new, mass readership was a visually arresting style which could make use of simple colour processes. For these, there were inventive prototypes among the later futurist books. Kruchenykh had produced the strikingly beautiful *Transrational book* (*Zaumnaya gniga*)[30] in 1915, illustrated with coloured lino-cuts by Rozanova. A real button is sewn on to a shiny red paper cut-out heart, glued to the cover which carries the false date, 1916. In that year one hundred copies of *Universal War* (*Vselenskaya voina*) were hand-made from pages of dark blue paper decorated with Rozanova's outstanding coloured collages.[31] Kruchenykh himself returned to both ideas in 1922 for *Transrationals* (*Zaumniki*) combining covers decorated with a lino-cut by Rodchenko and an original collage tipped in at the beginning of the book [colour plate 1i].

The cover design of *Transrationals* must be described as constructivist in style rather than futurist, yet, because different colours were used for different copies, it must, like the previous examples, have seemed too individual and personal to the artist concerned. However rebellious the first futurist books had been in 1912, as the years passed, the style, like every one that preceded it, was accepted and was no longer avant-garde. Only today, after a long interval, do the books seem remarkable in both graphic design and technique. All that is surprising is that their rediscovery has taken so long.

5

RUSSIAN FUTURIST BOOKS AND THE DEVELOPMENT OF AVANT-GARDE PAINTING

The years 1912 to 1916 were not only those when the main flow of futurist material was published, but also the period when the greatest advances in avant-garde art were made in Russia. This is no coincidence, for the books and journals record a struggle in art and literature by which painters and poets were attempting to create a truly Russian modern art.

Although it has been customary to give priority to the visual arts and connect poetic invention back to cubism as a major influence, the truth is not so simple. Interaction between poetic invention and the visual arts was significant but it was a two-way process. Writers picked on the usefulness of French cubism as a way of restructuring poetic language first, while the informed influence of cubism on the visual arts came after that of Italian futurist manifestos. Russian futurist books and journals confirm that two of the most original artists' inventions occurred as a result of the involvement of artists with writers, who had already made advances in their own field. Thus the illustrations he made for Kruchenykh's books document Larionov's investigation of several styles which contributed to his fully developed rayism, at a date rather later than has been put forward in recent years; while Malevich's invention of suprematism, which had a far wider influence than Larionov's rayism, occurred in 1915, by which time writers such as Mayakovsky and Khlebnikov had already achieved a mature avant-garde style.

At first, books and journals provided a vehicle for new poetry and illustrations and theoretical articles about art, as well as literary manifestos, but later, as has been outlined in the second chapter, Larionov wrote his own small book *Rayism* (*Luchizm*), illustrated with reproductions of work in the new style [18, 56]. Malevich followed this example, first with a pamphlet about suprematism and then with a book, *From Cubism and Futurism to Suprematism: new painterly realism* (*Ot kubizma i futurizma k suprematizmu: novyi zhivopisnyi realizm*), which included two illustrations and was published by November 1916 [79, 80]. Instead of examining them in isolation, or only in the context of the artist's work, they repay consideration in the wider connotation of futurist publications.

These have proved to be of the utmost historical importance, for with the establishment of very precise dates of issue, they provide an independent chronology which corrects the muddles which have arisen in the last twenty-five years, when artists competed to prove that they had been the first to make abstract art. In this respect it is necessary particularly to cite Larionov, for when general interest was suddenly roused by his rayist work towards the end of his life in Paris, he became determined to make out that he had invented non-figurative art before Kandinsky by whom an abstract water-colour, dated 1910 (a date subsequently discredited), had been found.[1] Larionov added new dates to early work and may even have painted new versions of previous compositions and altered them. Unfortunately, this has had the effect of making all his paintings less credible and it is lucky that futurist books reveal some of his strongest work and provide evidence for a revaluation of his importance.

In isolation, 'Rayist construction of a street' [56], which Larionov reproduced both in *Rayism* April 1913 and in *Donkey's Tail and Target* (*Oslinyi khvost i mishen*) about three months later, is a most fully worked-out drawing. It consists in a network of fine, crossing lines, probably with patches of colour at the points of intersection, which looks non-figurative. However, Larionov gave it a title and he may not have intended it to be seen as completely abstract, for in an article in *Donkey's Tail and Target* he explained:

> . . . the majority of dilettanti would think it very strange if objects as such were to disappear completely from a picture. Although all that they appreciate would still remain – colour, the painted surface, the structure of painted masses, texture. They would think it strange simply because we are accustomed to seeing what is of most value in painting in the context of objects.

He then explained his own position:

> We do not sense the object with our eye, as it is depicted conventionally in pictures and as a result of following this or that device; in fact we do not sense the object as such. We perceive a sum of rays proceeding from a source of light; these are reflected from the object and enter our field of vision.
>
> Consequently, if we wish to paint literally what we see, then we must paint the sum of rays reflected from the object. But in order to receive the total sum of rays from the desired object, we must select them deliberately – because together with the rays of the object being perceived, there also fall into our range of vision reflected reflex rays belonging to other nearby objects.

But this did not alter the fact for him that:

Painting is self-sufficient; it has its own forms, colour and timbre. Rayism is concerned with spatial forms that can arise from the intersection of the reflected rays of different objects, forms chosen by the artist's will.[2]

It is instructive to compare 'Rayist construction of a street' with a drawing which Larionov had made for Kruchenykh's first book of poems, published six months before [56, 57]. A full-page illustration on page 7 of *Old-time love* (*Starinnaya lyubov*) contains similar lines, running parallel and upwards, diagonally to the right, from near the bottom left-hand centre of the image. Under the heavy shading there gradually emerges the figure of a woman, holding an umbrella, standing stiffly in the foreground, while behind her, to the right, a man, wearing a hat, strides along the opposite side of the road (formed by two diagonals). On his right is a lamp-standard, emitting rays of light. Although figures have nearly vanished in 'Rayist construction of a street' the composition has some of the same structure. It includes similar diagonals, but with a strong grid, underlying the triangular clusters of rays. The illustrations for *Old-time love* represent Larionov's closest approach to Italian futurism, though, in a typical

56. Reproduction of 'Rayist construction of a street, 1912' by M. Larionov, included in *Rayism, 1913*, and *Donkey's Tail and Target, 1913*.

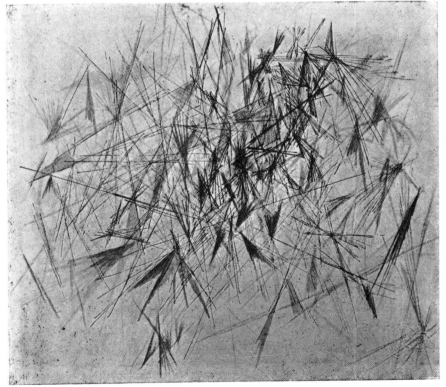

gesture, Larionov used the nude as subject – probably because the Italians had demanded 'for ten years, the total suppression of the nude in painting'.[3]

Although the stream of lines which overlay and hide the figures can be interpreted as lines of force, like the ones Boccioni was using, Larionov would probably have described them as an early form of rayism.[4] But other illustrations published between October 1912 and April 1913 confirm that he explored several modern as well as primitive styles, while developing rayism. Although it could be argued that Larionov made these illustrations many years before and only published them that winter, study of the sequence of books belies the idea: so strong was his collaboration with Kruchenykh at the time, that spontaneity of expression is one of the most striking features.

A rich record of Larionov's experiments are his lithographs in *Worldbackwards* (*Mirskontsa*), of December 1912. In 'Street Noises' [58], identifiable by its later titled reprint, Larionov depicts another urban scene, marrying primitive imagery to clusters of rays; treating the subject both realistically and conceptually by giving the same scale to a bar of music and to the man driving a donkey-cart. The musical notes may represent the call of the man, or sounds carried by the telegraph wires. In contrast, another lithograph, 'Woman at a café table' [59], again identifiable from the titled reprint in *Donkey's Tail and Target*, shows a woman's figure with her arms on the table, treated in a cubistic way, but with rays clustered at points of intersection.

57. *Old-time Love*, 1912: p. 7, drawing by M. Larionov.

58. *Worldbackwards*, 1912: leaf 7, 'Street Noises' by M. Larionov; lithograph.

59. *Donkey's Tail and Target*, 1913: reproduction of 'Woman at a cafe table, 1912' by M. Larionov from *Worldbackwards* 1912; size of this image, 9 x 7 cm. and of original, 18.4 x 13 cm.

Дама за столикомъ 1912 г.

60. *Worldbackwards*, 1912: leaf 32, drawing by M. Larionov to be 'read' either vertical or horizontal; here reproduced with book turned sideways; lithograph.

In an extreme case in *Worldbackwards*, Larionov's rays take on new meaning in a lithograph which, at first sight, contains borrowings from his paintings of soldiers' subjects – sabres and graffiti. Here it is reproduced with the book turned sideways [60] which is reasonable because Larionov has written his name along the spine edge (though his signature is unfortunately not visible in the copy of the book in the British Library). In this position the imagery can be interpreted as paleolithic. Small stick figures are taken from arctic or aboriginal sources; sabres become prehistoric spear sharpeners; long rays represent the incisions made on the rocks over many cave paintings; the black figure alone on the right-hand side is a prehistoric figure or sculpture.[5] Such an interpretation fits the paradoxical title, *Worldbackwards*, and is consistent with Livshits' recollections of staying with the Burliuks and trying to portray a 'chest of drawers as a Bushman'; Vladimir Burliuk was fascinated at that time by Neanderthal man.[6] (There were already plenty of fine books in print recording cave paintings of many kinds and at his death Larionov's library still contained a number of early books and pamphlets on archaeological and ethnological subjects.)[7] At this time, too, Khlebnikov wrote a poem entitled 'A Shaman and a Venus' and the marriage of the most modern with the most ancient was a general pre-occupation of the poets and painters, whose unique approach was called *budet-lyanstvo* by Livshits in his memoirs, to make clear its difference from *futurizm*.

In the light of his modern 'cave-painting', Larionov's next illustrations for Kruchenykh take on new significance: an illustration for *Pomade* (*Pomada*) entitled 'Lady with a hat', [colour plate 5], consists of a few rays, revealing

61. Reproduction of 'Portrait (ahead of a rayist construction), 1912' by M. Larionov, included in *Donkey's Tail and Target*.

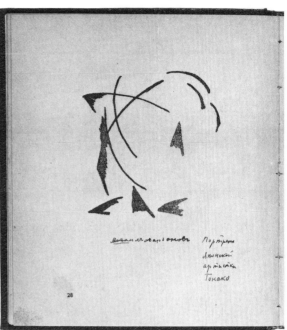

62. *A Trap for Judges 2*, 1913:
'Rayist portrait of
Nataliya Goncharova'
by M. Larionov,
printed on light blue paper,
opp. p. 43.

63. *A Trap for Judges 2*, 1913:
'Portrait of the Japanese *artiste*
Hanako' by M. Larionov,
printed on light blue paper,
opp. p. 28.

shoulder, neck and head surmounted by an elaborate arrangement like a wigwam, with overlapping strokes, for the hat. He used the schema again in paintings of heads, at least one of which, (now in the study collection of the Museum of Modern Art, New York), seems to represent an ancient Russian field spirit, traditionally represented as a kind of scarecrow made of straw.[8]

Larionov uses rays to link modern and ancient subject matter: rayism is shown to have validity as a method of modern art with roots in the distant past. Yet the extreme simplification of lines, used in such a basic way, was not arrived at by leaving out details, as a sequence of heads reproduced in futurist books demonstrates. Larionov is seen to have begun with a conventional, almost 'readable' image in 'Woman's portrait (ahead of a rayist construction)' [61] reproduced in *Donkey's Tail and Target* as well as in his biography. Instead of laying a grid over the face, (as an academically trained artist might have done with a study), he has picked out salients, which he has begun to explore with lines which form facets – this is particularly obvious on the right-hand side, and in the nose area. He has used shading, which normally conveys depth, but seems to have changed his mind and begun to extend some of the lines to unite the head with the background. Then he has strengthened some of the shading marks, so that they fan out from angles formed by the lines, on a smaller scale than the similar marks in the 'Woman at a café table' discussed above [59]. At first, this 'Woman's portrait' seems more naïve than 'Woman at a café table', yet it is less derivative, more original, for the lines begin to detach as a screen in front of the face, tentatively becoming the 'sum of rays . . . reflected from the object.'[9]

In the rayist portrait of Goncharova [62], which was reproduced first in *A Trap for Judges 2* (*Sadok sudei 2*) at the end of February, he takes the idea still further in a more complicated portrait, which appears to be three-quarter length. Although residual shoulders and arm seem relatively clear, the head seems to have disappeared entirely in favour of 'the intersection of the reflected rays of different objects, forms chosen by the artist's will'.[10] In total contrast, Larionov's 'Portrait of the Japanese *artiste* [actress] Hanako' was reproduced in the same book [63]. Here the head is suggested by the fewest possible lines, with some additional solids. The actress had fascinated Rodin in Paris, because of the extreme mobility of her features:[11] Larionov has presented a minimal record, to be filled in by the viewer's imagination. Yet, the choice of lines and their relation to the white page is extremely subtle, it is more 'readable' than the more advanced rayism of the portrait of Goncharova.

It seems that Larionov did not arrive at rayism to the exclusion of other interests. The 'Portrait of the Japanese *artiste* Hanako' makes an interesting antithesis to the head on the lithographed cover of *Half-alive* (*Poluzhivoi*), also of February, where in a negative image dense black takes the place of white [13]. Inside the book, figures are made of lines, rather than rays: on successive pages a nude is subjected to progressive discontinuity into marks which finally become increasingly like those of Chinese calligraphy [14, 15]. The parts of the nude take on the disjointing of the single letters of each handwritten word as the visual image is progressively more broken. It is as though the artist is exploring the extent to which deformation can be taken if the brain is still to be allowed to 'read' a figure. Full-page figures are constructed with angry, calligraphic strokes to match the violence of the poem [16].

From his theoretical exposition, it is not possible to understand quite why Larionov should have explored so many different kinds of primitive art while he was developing rayism, but his ideas were not entirely original. Points which had been made in two theoretical articles published a year before, help elucidate his standpoint. In the first and second journals of the Union of Youth, (*Soyuz molodezhi 1 i 2*), two parts of an article, 'The Principles of the New Art', had appeared (in April and June 1912) under the pseudonym Vladimir Markov.[12] The author, Voldemārs Matvejs, had first and foremost extolled chance, which he associated as a principle of creation with the East and with *nonconstructiveness*; in contrast, he noted that Europe has depended on logic, rationality and *constructiveness*. Paradoxically, while citing Chinese culture as one that values chance, he told a story which Larionov repeated, that Chinese artists were required to produce variations on the art of the past three thousand years and that they valued imitation and free copying very highly. This is one of the principal characteristics of Larionov's graphic works: influences from Chinese calligraphy, 'monuments of the stone age, of hunting people, preserved in caves', (a quotation from Markov's article), all fed into Larionov's own style, rayism, which he developed side by side with experiments in primitive art.

In this way, Larionov's rayism and primitive art can be seen to be close to the concerns of the poets: his figure of Akhmet [3] in *Worldbackwards* is the subject of Kruchenykh's poem written in child-like, rubber-stamped letters [colour plate 3]. Much of the contents of this book looks back to an earlier article, published by Nikolai Kulbin in *Impressionists' Studio* (*Studiya impressionistov*) in 1910, in which he wrote:

> Not everyone has the gift of reading the rudiments of the art created by the most beautiful of animals – primitive man and our children – although it is simpler.[13]

The title of Kulbin's article was 'Free Art as the Basis of Life' and David Burliuk praised Larionov's 'free drawing' in an article on 'Cubism' in *A Slap in the Face of Public Taste* (*Poshchechina obshchestvennomu vkusu*), January 1912.[14] He also singled out Kandinsky's work for the same characteristic.

In their most extreme form, both Larionov's rayism and Kandinsky's 'Improvisations' and 'Compositions' were, according to the Soviet historian Nikolai Khardzhiev, received as non-figurative when they were first exhibited in Russia, despite, or aside from, any theoretical expositions.[15]

Catalogues record that Larionov exhibited his first rayist work in December 1912: the two pictures cited above at the Union of Youth exhibition in St Petersburg and 'Glass – rayist method' (now in the Guggenheim Museum, New York) at the World of Art exhibition in Moscow. The drawings reproduced in *Rayism* in April 1913, such as 'Rayist construction of a street' [56], were his most advanced essays in the style and were, of course, in a form far more accessible for study than the pictures he included in the Target exhibition in Moscow held in the same month. 'Portrait of a fool' reproduced in Zdanevich's biography a few months later, seems to underlie 'Blue rayism'[16] (Private collection, Paris) and was much more representational in its original state.

Backed up by the theoretical explanation, Larionov's rayist work seems to have been reflected in articles by poets about the new approach to writing: From the rather vague:

> And if *for the time being* even our lines are still marked with dirty stigmas of your 'common sense' and 'good taste', there tremble on them *for the first time* the summer lightnings of the New-coming Beauty of the Self-sufficient (self-centred) Word.[17]

in the manifesto 'A Slap in the Face of Public Taste,' one of the Hylaeans, Livshits, (who had not in fact signed the manifesto) was able to write confidently by the end of the summer:

> Here our poetry is free, and for the first time, we do not care whether it is realistic, naturalistic, or fantastic; except for its

starting point, it does not place itself in any relationships with the world and does not coordinate itself with it; all other crossing points of this poetry with the world are *a priori* accidental.[18]

Although applied to poetry and not to painting, the position resembles Larionov's, yet, Livshits' article, 'The liberation of the word' appeared in *The Croaked Moon (Dokhlaya luna)*, one of the first books to carry the word *Futuristy* as well as Hylaea, making absolutely clear the difference between his group and the '*Luchisty i Budushchniki*' – rayists and futurists (using the chosen Russian word) of Larionov's group.

But even before Larionov had published *Rayism*, Rozanova had described a different approach to the problem of abstraction in art. She put forward the theory of *bezpredmetnoe* art – non-figurative art, in 'The bases of the New Creation and the Reason why it is Misunderstood' in the *Union of Youth 3 (Soyuz molodezhi 3)* in March 1913. Here she established the following order in the process of creation:

1) Intuitive Principle
2) Individual transformation of the visible
3) Abstract creation.

64. *Union of Youth 3*, 1913: drawing by O. Rozanova on yellow, glazed paper, opp. p. 22; lithograph.

She argued:

> Only now does the artist create a Picture quite consciously not only by not copying nature, but also by subordinating the primitive conception of it to conceptions complicated by all the psychology of modern creative thought: what the artist sees + what he knows + what he remembers, etc.

But she rejected the 'nonconstructive' ideal which Markov had advocated and, drawing on her knowledge of modern western European art, she said:

> Only modern Art has advocated the full and serious importance of such principles as pictorial dynamism, volume and equilibrium, weight and weightlessness, linear and plane displacement, rhythm as a legitimate division of space, design, planar and surface dimension, texture, colour correlation and others. Suffice it to enumerate these principles that distinguish the New Art from the Old to be convinced that they are the Qualitative – and not just the quantitative – New Basis that proves the 'self-sufficient' significance of the New Art. They are principles hitherto unknown that signify the rise of a new era in creation – an era of purely artistic achievements.[19]

She draws the conclusion that these principles will bring about the 'absolute liberation of the Great Art of Painting.' In practice, she found the application difficult: the illustrations which she made for the journal do not fulfil her aims [64]. The great difficulties of pictorial abstraction can be seen in the attempt by Mayakovsky to make a 'senseless' drawing for *Service Book of the Three (Trebnik troikh)*, which was registered during the first week of April 1913 [65].

In contrast to Mayakovsky's drawing, one by David Burliuk printed in the same book is based on his interpretation of cubism, which he had set out in *A Slap in the Face of Public Taste* [66]. A nude shows a rather precise application: he has cut and shifted the parts into a new arrangement. Late in 1911 Burliuk had interpreted the cubist invention of multiple views of a single object to mean an object seen from all points of the compass, rather than from adjacent positions to the left and right of centre. He had begun to make pictures which can be turned and viewed any way up. (Livshits reproduced one of them in his memoirs.[20]) During 1913, Burliuk combined the idea with one taken from the technical manifesto of Italian futurist painting: 'Thus a running horse has not four legs, but twenty, and their movements are triangular.'[21] He made a literal interpretation in a series of drawings first reproduced in *A Trap for Judges 2*, in February [36, 37]. There, the parts of a horse and man look as though they

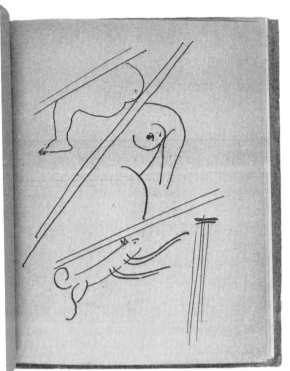

might have been first assembled out of gummed paper shapes, giving the added connotation of children's art.[22] In the most elaborate, the images are so fragmented that only two whole animals can be made out, other shapes no longer 'make sense'. However, a kind of 'sense' can be derived, because the composition is made up of elements, recognisable in other drawings in the series.

Burliuk's approach is utterly unlike any western European version of cubism and, indeed, were it not for his theoretical article, would not be connected with that movement. Yet here he hit on a device which was later on to prove most important in the development of abstract art. One of the illustrations was used on the poster advertising the futurist theatre productions later that year and, surprisingly, reproduced on the back cover of the book, *Victory over the Sun* (*Pobeda nad solntsem*). But (as has been noted in the chapter on theatre) the splitting apart of geometricised elements of the figure was a key factor of Malevich's revolutionary approach to costumes and lighting in the production of the opera and one which finally helped over the next two years to lead to his geometric, non-figurative style, suprematism. Throughout 1913 it is possible to establish a large number of ideas being expressed by the avant-garde of which he was a member, which caused Malevich later on to insist that the roots of suprematism were to be found in that year.[23]

Although in 1913 Larionov can be seen to have approached non-figuration in his rayist work, his example was not followed by other members of the avant-garde at the time. Indeed, Malevich, who had been an exhibitor at the Donkey's Tail in 1912 and also took part in the Target exhibition in April 1913, split with

65, 66. *The Service-book of the Three*, 1913: V. Mayakovsky, drawing for his poem 'Sign-board' (*'Vyveskam'*), opp. p. 42; lithograph. D. Burliuk, drawing of nude and dog, after p. 86.

67. *Explodity*, 1913: leaf 17, 'Simultaneous death of a man in an aeroplane and at the railway; by K. Malevich; lithograph 17.5 x 11 cm.

68. Reproduction of 'Aeroplane over the train, 1913' by N. Goncharova, included in *Donkey's Tail and Target*, 1913.

Larionov after the exhibition. The paintings he hung there reveal him to be much more concerned with volume and coloured areas than with line. He showed 'Knife-grinder/principle of flickering' for the first time, (a painting at the University of Yale Art Gallery, often reproduced). Before this, Malevich had been very close to Goncharova; for example, his painting 'Woman with buckets and child' (Stedelijk Museum, Amsterdam), which had been shown in Moscow at the turn of the year, is very close to her 'Peasants picking Apples', which Shevchenko reproduced in his *Principles of Cubism and other Contemporary Trends in Painting of all Ages and all Nations* (*Printsipy kubizma i drugikh sovremennykh*

techenii v zhivopisi vsekh vremen i narodov) during the summer, though the
lithograph was almost certainly an earlier work. The source for the curious
heads in both artists' work are stone sculptures from the dark ages, the *kamennye
baby* which fascinated Goncharova.[24] Although Malevich did not stop studying
the work of Goncharova and Larionov – especially their work reproduced in
publications – his own position changed very strongly away from theirs during
the remainder of the year.

One of the first lithographs which Malevich made for Kruchenykh was
included in *Explodity* (*Vzorval*) in June; it is inscribed along the side:
'Simultaneous death of a man in an aeroplane and at the railway' [67]. The
subject is again quite close to one which Goncharova had chosen for a painting:
'Aeroplane over the train'. It was reproduced in *Donkey's Tail and Target* and
even in the photograph [68] the train and aeroplane are fairly easily
recognisable, with the carriages of the train visually linked to houses beside the
track. Malevich gives his lithographic version a violent end; using Goncharova's
more readable aeroplane as a guide, his own can be seen to be twisted round,
apparently entangled in telegraph wires, which add another kind of
communication to the subject. Both artists have chosen subject-matter extolled
in Italian futurist manifestos, but Malevich seems to have carried representation
into new realms, even new dimensions and this acts as a reminder that his own
aims were becoming more precise and more metaphysical than those of Italian
artists or of Goncharova, more nearly related to ideas shared by Kruchenykh
and Matyushin.

A second lithograph by Malevich included in the same book is in total contrast
in subject and treatment, but much closer to the new point of view. It is called
'Prayer' and shows a calm, kneeling figure of a peasant woman, reduced to the
barest number of elements, linked to suggest a bowed head and a hand touching
the forehead, just beginning the movement of crossing herself [69]. Malevich
has not completed the outline of the figure but left a plane open to the white
background, to suggest the interpenetration of the figure by a world from
beyond, by another dimension, or higher intuition. It suggests, that, like
Kruchenykh, Malevich began to study a book from which Matyushin had
quoted in an article in March, *Tertium Organum* by P. D. Uspensky.[25]

In *Union of Youth 3*, Matyushin had linked this mystical treatise, published in
St Petersburg two years before, with *Du Cubisme* by Gleizes and Metzinger,
recently published in Paris.[26] Matyushin picked up a single, not very direct
reference to 'dimensions' in *Du Cubisme* and proceeded to identify the main
feature of cubism as a desire to reveal a fourth dimension. He may have relied on
accounts of talk in the studios in Paris, where artists discussed the subject a good
deal. It has been shown recently that some Parisian artists were fascinated by a
treatise written by a mathematician called Jouffret,[27] who had tried to show

how a fourth dimension, at right-angles to the familiar three, could be drawn by means of superimposed polyhedrons.[28] Following his own considerable studies on the subject, Matyushin jumped to the conclusion that they were interested in another method of revealing a fourth dimension, by using cubes to form a 'magic' figure called a tesseract. From *Tertium Organum* he excerpted Uspensky's quotations from *The Fourth Dimension* by Charles Howard Hinton in which this method had been set out some years before.[29]

For Matyushin, cubism assumed the role of a method of making art which could lead to a new awareness of a higher existence beyond the one we know, to be revealed by expanding the senses:

> Cubism set our consciousness on the path towards a new spatial conception . . . The direct representation of nature was finished.[30]

69. *Explodity*, 1914, second edition: leaf 19, 'Prayer', by K. Malevich; lithograph 17.5 x 11.6 cm., identical with one in first edition, 1913.

This quotation is from Matyushin's memoirs of 1934, but he embarked on the way in 1913, when, in September, in a preface for *The Three* (*Troe*) he wrote:

> And perhaps that day is not far off when the vanquished phantoms of three-dimensional space, of seemingly drop-like time, of melancholy causality and many other things will prove to be for all of us exactly what they are: the annoying bars of a cage in which the human spirit is imprisoned – and that's all.[31]

In the same book, Kruchenykh published 'New ways with the word – the language of man-of-the-future, the death of symbolism'. He too quoted from Uspensky:

> At the present moment we have three units of psychic life, sensation, perception, conception (with idea) and there is beginning to form a fourth unit, higher intuition.[32]

Uspensky had explained that higher intuition is

> possible of attainment through the emotion attendant upon creation – in painters, musicians and poets. Art in its highest manifestations is a path to cosmic consciousness.[33]

During the summer, Kruchenykh had begun to see the 'language of man-of-the-future' as the 'WORD BROADER THAN SENSE' – the climax of his article 'New ways with the word'. For Kruchenykh the 'man-of-the-future', *Budetlyanin*, (a word made up by Khlebnikov) was like a hopeful Platonist, expecting to experience a higher state of consciousness. The 'WORD BROADER THAN SENSE' was not *non*sense, but the extension of our ordinary awareness, by art created outside the accepted categories of logic. In a literal way the world was to be turned upside down and during the summer when Kruchenykh, Matyushin and Malevich were staying in Finland, photographs of them were taken in front of a background, literally turned upside-down.[34]

Kruchenykh had begun to choose words 'broader than sense' for the titles of his books after his move to St Petersburg. No longer did he use straightforward descriptions like *Half-alive* (*Poluzhivoi*) or *Hermits* (*Pustynniki*) but experimented with double meanings derived from unexpected juxtapositions. For example, *Bukh lesinnyi* (published in June) is virtually untranslatable, for the usual *A Forestly Rapid* leaves out the many meanings implicit in the non-sense title. *Bukh* is close to the German or English word 'book', and to the Russian *dukh*, meaning a spirit, as well as suggesting the splosh of a heavy object falling into water. The *les* of the first syllable of the second word literally means a wood, but the unexpected addition of *sinnyi* adds blue to the meaning, suggesting a pine forest. Rozanova has included these ideas on the cover design [70].[35]

70. *A Forestly Rapid*, 1913: hand-written poems by A. Kruchenykh and V. Khlebnikov. Lithographed cover design by O. Rozanova on green paper (faded), 14.5 x 9.5 cm.

Intentional ambiguity is likewise the hall-mark of Kruchenykh's poetry experiments. During the summer he developed the *zaum* language which he had already used in a poem which became his own favourite, '*Dir bul shchyl*' (made-up words) first printed in *Pomade*.[36] But he began to modify this language, attempting to achieve a modern version of *glossolalia*. The cover drawing which Kulbin made for *Explodity* shows a stick figure standing in a cube (perhaps a pulpit) gesticulating at an angry audience – also abbreviated into stick figures – who wave their fists and brawl [26]. Similar figures recur within the book, edging a page with words arranged as shouts emanating from them [71]. The words are 'BROADER THAN SENSE', *zaum*, intended to be a universal language for the future man, aspiring to higher intuition. So, although Kulbin's cover drawing might be interpreted as an ordinary futurist gathering of a type familiar in Italy, it could also be intended to portray an inspired religious congregation, whose *glossolalia*, speaking in tongues, Kruchenykh described as a precursor of *zaum*.

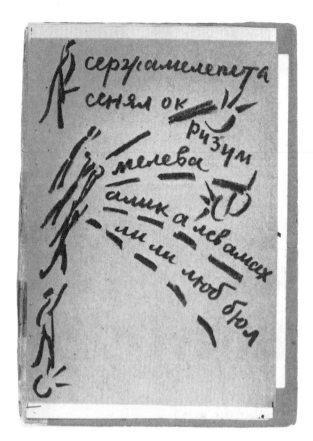

Visual ambiguity is included in an image in the same book, following Kruchenykh's announcement: 'On 27 April at 3 pm I mastered all languages in a momentary flash. Such is a poet of modern times.'[37] The artist Natan Altman drew for him marks which are imitation Hebrew letters, but also form the colloquial Russian word *shish* – fig – and resemble a cluster of musical notes [72].[38]

In the context of these double meanings, the two lithographs by Malevich included in *Explodity* [67, 69] appear almost conventional – at least they represent experiments in style in art in much the same way that a poem might show literary innovations, to a less extreme degree than Kruchenykh's *zaum*. Yet, when in November Malevich exhibited four oil paintings of subjects which he had used in lithograph form in Kruchenykh's books, he bracketed three of these titles in the catalogue *zaumnyi realizm*, so he evidently intended a close connection with the literary experiments. The four subjects were: 'Peasant woman with buckets' (Museum of Modern Art, New York); 'Completed portrait of Ivan Vasilevich Klyun' (Russian Museum, Leningrad); 'Face of a peasant girl' (Stedelijk Museum, Amsterdam); and 'Reaping woman' (whereabouts unknown) which he described as 'cubo-futurist realism'. All are subjects which Malevich worked on during the year when he was most closely connected with Hylaea and, except for the portrait of his friend, the artist Ivan Klyun, they are of

71, 72. *Explodity*, 1914, second edition: leaf 24, lithographed page of *zaum* writing by A. Kruchenykh, figures by N. Kulbin, 16.4 x 11.7. Leaf 29, image by N. Altman, lithographed by Svet, 17.5 x 11.3; both identical with leaf in first edition, 1913.

73. *Let's Grumble*, 1913:
'Peasant woman goes for water'
by K. Malevich;
second lithograph on white paper,
tipped in before text,
17.4 x 11 cm.

peasants, a preoccupation which he linked in his autobiography to his friendship with Goncharova.[39]

Malevich's lithograph 'Peasant woman goes for water' was included in the second of Kruchenykh's books published after his move to St Petersburg, *Let's Grumble* (*Vozropshchem*) [73]. In the lithograph, the planes have a transparent quality which allows the woman's figure to merge with her surroundings, it has none of the sharpness of definition of the oil painting of the same title.

This is also the case with the lithograph 'Portrait of a builder completed' [colour plate 20], and the related painting, 'Completed portrait of Ivan Klyun', on to which Malevich later added the date 1911. The lithograph version seems originally to have had the title *Portret stroitelya* – Portrait of a builder – written in the same way as *Molitva* – Prayer – had been written on an earlier lithograph [69]. The word *usovershenstvovan* – completed – may have been added as an afterthought. Malevich was unusually precise about the titles of all the lithographs he provided for Kruchenykh: the subject of even the most obscure drawing is systematically identified by writing as though he was determined that however unfamiliar the style he adopted, it should not be misinterpreted, or seen as non-figurative. The reason for the added words in this case was that he had already exhibited an earlier version of 'Portrait of Ivan Klyun' at the Union of Youth exhibition of 1912–13, (reproduced in a review early in 1913[40]), so the new version needed explanation. The planes of the earlier head, have been shifted: the right-hand upper part of the head is opened up to reveal another world within, perhaps representing the 'higher intuition' achieved by Ivan Klyun. This idea must have continued to have force, for at a memorial ceremony after Malevich's death, a friend read a poem including the line:

Give me your eyes! I want to open a window on my nut![41]

In two illustrations by Vladimir Burliuk, included in *A Trap for Judges 2* in February, the one most recognisable as a head had included unexpected 'windows' leading to a different world, beyond the one familiar to us [74].

74, 75. *A Trap for Judges 2*, 1913: head by Vladimir Burliuk, printed in black and grey on light blue paper, following p. 107. Head-form by Vladimir Burliuk, printed on light blue paper, opp. p. 4.

Whereas eye, ear and nose are easily identifiable, the other related composition is totally abstracted, though based on a head form [75]. A rough square is divided by straight lines into a number of crudely geometric forms arranged so that recession is suggested in an ambiguous way. Without describing an object, Vladimir has constructed a picture using recognised pictorial language – light, shadow, spatial definition, line plane and texture, in such a way that an analogy is suggested with a familiar idea, thus making possible the imagination of a head form. In contrast, Malevich makes the image of Ivan Klyun much more concrete and less abstract.

Malevich's 'Portrait of a builder completed' [colour plate 20] which was included in *Piglets* (*Porosyata*) (registered in mid-August) makes an interesting comparison with a slightly later illustration by Larionov for Bolshakov's poem *Le Futur*. There he depicted a woman's head, overlaid by lines forming rays, with a small cyclist drawn on her cheek. Strangely, in each head there is a connection with a phrase from the Italian futurist technical manifesto of painting. In the case of the Malevich:

> We affirm once again that a portrait, in order to be a work of art, cannot and must not resemble the sitter and that the painter carries within him the landscape he wishes to produce.

and the Larionov:

> How often have we not seen on the cheek of the person with whom we were talking, the horse which passes at the end of the street.[42]

Each artist has created a new interpretation of the western European avant-garde, using devices from French cubism – Klyun's shifted eye, the letters and numbers overlying Larionov's outlined head – as formal aids in their rival explorations to find a Russian modern style. In the woman's head, Larionov has both simplified and taken further his earlier explorations of line as a means of making images; in the 'Portrait of a builder completed' Malevich has rationalised his previous use of volumes so evident in the lithograph 'Peasant woman' on the cover of the same book [colour plate 19].

The head of a peasant woman must have been an important subject to Malevich, for in mid-September, a month after *Piglets* came out, a more finished drawing of the same subject was reproduced (photographically) in *The Three* [76]. Like the builder, 'Peasant woman' shows a close-up view of the head: she has a typical peasant scarf tied under her chin and represents another view of the profile woman in 'Prayer' or 'Peasant woman goes for water' [69, 73]. In its final development in the oil painting, the interlocking, overlapping forms of

'Face of a peasant girl' are created in a sculptural way and the colours bear out the idea of metallic forms. The head is static and peaceful in all versions, compared with contemporary figures of reapers by Malevich.

Although the painting 'Woman reaper' shown at the Union of Youth exhibition in November is not identified, Malevich treated the subject in a

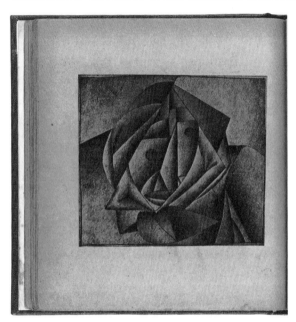 

lithograph glued to the cover of *The Word as such* (*Slovo kak takovoe*) [colour plate 22], and in a drawing reproduced in *The Three* [77]. Like the head of the peasant woman, the two figures of reapers are composed of geometric volumes, sometimes folded inside each other and sometimes overlapping. But none of the geometric cones has a precise, finite form, for the lines at the angles continue into the surrounding spaces, creating new, unfinished parts of geometric bodies. Although *The Word as such* was not registered until mid-October, the lithograph is on similar greenish paper to those of *Piglets*, registered two months before [colour plates 19 and 20]. The drawing of the reaper in *The Three* in many ways seems more advanced: the parts of the figure are more clearly defined, but at the same time more logically shifted or displaced. The counterchange between darks and lights even seems to approach the *'Contrastes des formes'* with which Fernand Léger was experimenting.[43] The reaper on the cover of *The Word as such* may well have been made earlier, at the same time as the lithographs for *Piglets*.

The most elaborate and original drawing reproduced in *The Three* shows an aviator, set among the parts of his aeroplane, which have acquired autonomy as geometric solids [78]. They represent the disintegration of known space, which

76, 77. *The Three*, 1913: reproduction of a drawing related to 'Head of a Peasant Girl' by K. Malevich, opp. p. 71. Reproduction of a drawing of a 'Woman Reaper' by K. Malevich, opp. p. 50.

78. *The Three*, 1913:
reproduction of a drawing
of a 'Pilot' [?] by K. Malevich,
opp. p. 82.

they share with ingredients from literature, full-stops, commas hurling through
an instant in cosmic space. Malevich has captured a line from the poem by Elena
Guro printed on the page opposite:

> the visionary who has been set on fire with such terrible
> sonorous light.[44]

Yet, remarkable though this drawing is, and close in spirit to lines spoken by the
Elocutionist in Act II of Kruchenykh's 'Victory over the Sun' –

> liberated from the weight of earth's gravitation we
> whimsically arrange our belongings as if a rich kingdom
> were moving[45]

the composition is fully three-dimensional. It is even more so than the lithograph
'Arithmetic' in which Malevich had combined cabalistic numbers with
overlapping triangles and punctuation marks in *Let's Grumble* in June [48].

   In retrospect, during 1913, Malevich can be seen to have had only one serious
Russian rival for primacy in the field of painting. This was Larionov, whose

versatile experiments perhaps inspired Malevich, not only in the similar range of formal discoveries displayed by his lithographs, but in more precise ways.

Especially influential were Larionov's illustrations for Bolshakov's poem *Le Futur*. Among the lithographs is one showing the parts of a clock: a minute-hand is left incomplete, with a second-hand joined by arrows directing time through space simultaneously in several directions. In spite of remaining apart from the Hylaeans, Larionov here approached very closely to Kruchenykh's idea of 'whimsical' arrangement. Later in the autumn, with Zdanevich, Larionov explained why he and his friends painted images on their own faces giving a reason surprisingly close to Kruchenykh's point of view: '. . . we want to herald the unknown, to rearrange life and to bear man's multiple soul to the upper reaches of reality'.[46]

In the head with a cyclist drawn on her cheek, referred to above, Larionov used letters superimposed on various parts of the page, which gives it something of the complexity of Kruchenykh's *zaum* book titles. His choice of 3r. BL and YA together convey the information – three roubles, but alogically, they can have other interpretations. 'BL' is enigmatic, though the letters can sound the now old-fashioned Russian word for 'bill'; *Ya* is simply the Russian word for 'I'; there is even the suggestion of the Russian word for a prostitute, conveyed by the letters BLYa and Larionov made a series of paintings of prostitutes at this time. Larionov claimed that the inspiration behind the use of letters by himself and Goncharova in their paintings of the period, was the signboards to be found above Russian shops. But, like their insistence that cubism could be found in ancient Russian sculptures, it is open to the obvious criticism that, even if such local inspiration was to hand, artists did not think of using it until the French cubists had led the way. The use of letters in drawings in spatial arrangements to suggest alternative meanings, pioneered in Russia by Larionov and Goncharova, was fruitfully borrowed by Malevich.

Unfortunately, by reference to futurist illustrations, it is not possible to demonstrate the way Malevich arranged parts of words to give punning meanings, for he used them in a series of 'Eclipse' paintings which he made in 1914 after he had stopped contributing to books. Parallel to overlapping letters, and images, Malevich began to allow flattened, coloured geometric planes to occlude his forms. He had used such shapes in his set design for 'Victory over the Sun' reproduced in December 1913 on the front cover of the libretto [35]; in it the structure is much simpler than his earlier work. Forms are contained in a superimposed, opened-out box-like space, which recedes or comes forward in optical illusion; dark shapes have irregular geometricised forms, but do not yet occlude other, more representational shapes – they simply share the space.

The same is not true of a design which Livshits reproduced in his memoirs.[47] Unlike any other known drawing for the opera, Malevich does not there use a framed structure: the drawing is vertical, not horizontal, in format, and seems to show a sequence of 'pictures' – tiny, stick-like people are silhouetted in some compartments, while other compartments are occupied by words, numbers, clouds, guns – ingredients of the text of the opera. But, the separate compartments are not regularly arranged, some overlap others, they vary in size and shape and the whole drawing is overlaid with several of the main compositional lines of Malevich's genuinely cubist works, like the painting 'Musical-instrument/lamp' (Stedelijk Museum, Amsterdam) which he exhibited at the time of the production of 'Victory over the Sun'. But even more mysterious in the design reproduced by Livshits, are the frankly suprematist superimposed elements – a black rectangle, a square and some diagonal black forms, related both to the 'Eclipse' paintings and to the fully suprematist pictures which he exhibited in December 1915.

This set design remains an enigma: but Nikolai Khardzhiev recently clarified the relationship of the opera to Malevich's development of suprematism:

> . . . the first purely suprematist construction followed a date in May 1915 when Malevich created a series of drawings for a second (unrealised) publication of the play by A. Kruchenykh. On 27 May 1915 he sent M. Matyushin a drawing for the curtain – portraying a black square – Malevich wrote: 'This drawing will have great significance for painting, for what was done unconsciously, is now giving extraordinary results.'[48]

The key (previously un-noted) information in this passage is that the drawings were 'created' and therefore *new*: thus arguments about whether the black square was used as a curtain in the original performance are irrelevant. There is no reason to suppose that the drawing reproduced by Livshits is not a later drawing, which would account for the innovations.

As has been previously mentioned, Malevich's exclusively geometric style, suprematism, was explained in two publications of which the second includes the earliest printed minimal paintings: the black square and the black circle [79, 80]. In 1919 he published a full visual record entitled *Suprematism 34 drawings* (*Suprematizm 34 risunka*).[49] Included among the lithographs (the finest examples of autolithography in Russian books[50]) are some which are related to drawings which Malevich made during 1915 for paintings exhibited in the Zero-ten show, at which he launched his invention. Unlike some other artists, he gave titles to the non-figurative works, no longer written on them as on the lithographs for futurist books, but not to be ignored.

He was not imitating the Ego-futurist poet, who, in 1913, had published poem no 15, 'Poem of the End' ('*Poema kontsa*'), which consisted of the title printed on a blank page. The poem, by Vasilisk Gnedov, was included in a book with the title *Death to Art* (*Smert iskusstvu*), and was described in the preface:

> 'Poem of the End' is actually 'Poem of Nothing', a zero, as it
> is drawn graphically.[51]

Malevich's suprematism was based on a less negative zero – on the notion that it is possible to transcend zero, to descend to 0 and go through, beyond it:

79, 80. *From Cubism and Futurism to Suprematism: New Painterly Realism*, 3rd printing, 1916: text by K. Malevich. 'Black Square' and 'Black Circle' by K. Malevich, lithographs tipped in between pp. 28–9 and 12–13.

> But I am transfigured in the zero of forms and have gone
> beyond 0–1. Believing that cubo-futurism has fulfilled its
> marks, I go on to suprematism, to the new pictorial realism,
> to non-figurative creation.

and

> the word suprematism stands for the championship (i.e. the
> supremacy) of colour problems.[52]

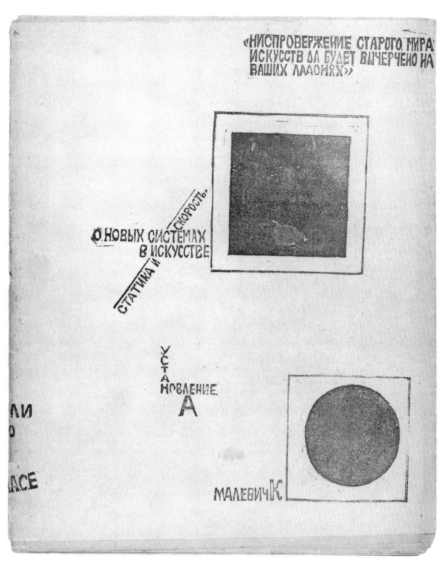

81. *On New Systems in Art*, 1919: hand-written text by K. Malevich. Lithographed cover design by El Lissitzky (continued on back cover which is continuous with the front).

Although Russian futurist books do not exemplify this revolutionary stance in Malevich's own work, early in 1916 what could be described as a 'zaum-suprematist' book was published. Kruchenykh paid tribute to Malevich's invention in a collection of poems under the title *Universal War* (*Vselenskaya voina*) in which words gave place to collages made by Rozanova, who had exhibited representational work in the Zero-ten exhibition. On sheets of deep blue paper are pasted shapes cut in clear, coloured tissue paper, sometimes contrasted with pieces of coloured cloth or other papers. These visual poems were only to be challenged (no doubt, unconsciously) by Matisse's cut paper compositions forty years later, but have never been excelled in book form.[53] Rozanova's collages have the spontaneity and freedom and, above all, the colour which was characteristic of Malevich's paintings at the Zero-ten exhibition.

Zero-ten was subtitled the Last Futurist Exhibition. Malevich's friends had been dismayed at his desire to reject the label futurist. In a letter to Matyushin he had relayed the dilemma experienced by his fellow exhibitors:

> . . . neither are we Futurists any more, but we still don't know how to define ourselves and we've had too little time to think about it.[54]

Rozanova, who had early shown herself a serious student of the problems of abstraction in art, very quickly seized on the possibilities of Malevich's suprematist solution. Her untimely death in 1918 cut short her experiments.

In the field of book illustration, perhaps the most remarkable use of Malevich's ideas is to be found in El Lissitzky's work in Vitebsk, beginning with his cover design for *On New Systems in Art* (*O novykh sistemakh v iskusstve* [81].[55] Conceived in Vitebsk in 1920, though printed in Berlin in 1922 is his most original story: 'Of Two Squares' (*Pro dva kvadrata*). Using typographical arrangements rather like those pioneered in Kamensky's ferro-concrete poems, Lissitzky linked one page to the next; yet the words are hardly important, each page is dominated by suprematist forms initiated by Malevich, arranged within a finely outlined square.

It will be argued that *Of Two Squares* is a constructivist book – and so it is. For Lissitzky has in a sense betrayed Malevich, the reader is told:

> Don't read, get paper, rods, blocks, set them out, paint them, build

and on the final page:

> This is the end – let's go on.[56]

But, by 1920, Malevich himself had begun to construct three-dimensional 'architectons', suprematist architectural models, planned for the 'man-of-the-present' to inhabit. The 'man-of-the-future' who had inspired revolutionary changes in the forms of art, was now the man of the present, or, perhaps, the man of the past. The new art, whether suprematist, realistic, constructivist or productivist was all a product of the changes wrought by futurist ideas. Indeed the term was not yet abandoned.

Much of this account has been devoted to the year 1913, but from all the inventions of that year stemmed avant-garde art, often following in the wake of avant-garde poetry. The two Strong men of the future country who had torn the curtain at the beginning of 'Victory over the Sun', reappeared on the stage at the end of the opera to say:

everything is good that
has a good beginning
   and doesn't have an end
the world will die but for us there is no
   end![57]

NOTES

Abbreviations:

VM   Vladimir Markov: *Russian Futurism, A History*. London, Macgibbon and Kee, 1969
JB   John E. Bowlt (editor): *Russian Art of the Avant-garde: Theory & Criticism 1902–34. The Documents of 20th-century Art*. N.Y., Viking Press, 1976
NKh Nikolai Khardzhiev, Kazimir Malevich and Mikhail Matyushin: *K istorii russkogo avangarda / The Russian Avant-garde*. Stockholm, Hylaea Prints, 1976

1: INTRODUCTION

1. Maurice Denis: 'Définition du néo-traditionnisme' in *Art et Critique*, 23 and 30 August 1890; republished in *Théories (1890–1910): du symbolisme et de Gauguin vers un nouvel ordre classique*, Paris, Bibl. de l'Occident, 1912, p. 1.

2. Camilla Gray: *The Great Experiment in Russian Art 1863–1922*, London, Thames and Hudson, 1962.

3. *VM*: pp. 7–8.

4. For different accounts of Mayakovsky, see Edward J. Brown: *Mayakovsky – A Poet in the Revolution*, Princeton University Press, 1973, and *Vladimir Mayakovsky: Innovator*, trans. from Russian by Alex Miller, Moscow, Progress, 1976.

5. English translation from R. W. Flint: *Marinetti. Selected writings*, London, Secker and Warburg, 1972, pp. 352–3.

6. Benedikt Livshits: *Polutoraglazyi strelets*, Leningrad, 1933. Translated into French: *L'Archer à un oeil et demi* by Valentine and Jean-Claude Marcadé, Lausanne, L'Age d'Homme, 1971, and into English: *The One and a Half-Eyed Archer* by John E. Bowlt, Newtonville, Mass., Oriental Research Partners, 1977.

7. Viktor Shklovsky: *Mayakovsky and his Circle*, trans. and ed. by Lily Feiler, N.Y., Pluto Press, 1974, p. 76. Russian source given: V. Mayakovsky, 'O raznykh Mayakovskikh' *Pol. sob. soch. Mayakovskogo, v 13 tom.* ed. V. Katanyan, Moscow, 1955, vol. 1, p. 344.

8. Quoted by Robert Lord: *Russian and Soviet Literature. An introduction*, England, Kahn and Averill, 1972, p. 43 (no Russian source given).

9. *VM*: p. 28 Russian source given: 'Vel. Khlebnikov – osnovatel budetlyan . . .' *Kniga i revolyutsiya* no. 9–10 (1922), p. 25.

10. E. Nizen: *O Kubizme*, St P. Zhuravl, 1913. M.V.: *Sovremennye problemy*, Moscow, 1913.

11. Mayakovsky's poem from *A Trap for Judges 2* (*Sadok sudei 2*) is transliterated by Troels Andersen: *Malevich*, Stedelijk Museum Amsterdam, 1970, p. 25 and discussed by Edward J. Brown: *Mayakovsky – A Poet in the Revolution*, op. cit., pp. 79–80.

12. Nikolai Kulbin read aloud Kandinsky's Russian text, 'O dukhovnom v iskusstve', at the All-Russian Congress of Artists in St Petersburg, 29 and 31 December 1911 a few weeks after the publication of *Über das Geistige in der Kunst*, Munich, 1911.

13. Both Malevich and Tatlin exhibited their non-figurative paintings and sculpture at an exhibition entitled 'Zero-Ten: the last futurist exhibition' held at the Dobychina gallery in Petrograd in December 1915.

14. In *Pomade* (*Pomada*) February 1913, the first line was hand-written 'Dir bul shchyl'. The poem was subsequently printed in *The Word as such* (*Slovo kak takovoe*) as '*dyr bul shchyl*' and repeated in *Te li le* with new variations.

2: POETS AND PAINTERS
– A CHRONOLOGY

1. *Spring* (*Vesna*), published by N. G. Shebuev for three months in St Petersburg in 1908.

2. This date was published by Tatiana Loguine: *Gontcharova et Larionov, cinquante ans à Saint Germain-des-Prés*. Paris, Klincksieck, 1971, p. 13, note 9.

3. See chapter 1, note 6.

4. The contents of this catalogue and many others referred to in this book are listed by Valentine Marcadé in the second appendix to her useful book: *Le Renouveau de l'Art Pictural Russe 1863–1914*, Lausanne, L'Age d'Homme, 1971.

5. *Der Blaue Reiter*, ed. V. Kandinsky and F. Marc, Munich, Piper, 1912. English translation edited by Klaus Lankheit: *The Blaue Reiter Almanac. The Documents of 20th-century Art*, London, Thames and Hudson, 1974.

6. See N. Khardzhiev: 'Mayakovsky i zhivopis', *Mayakovsky: materialy i issledovaniya*, Moscow, 1940, p. 343.

7. Only the name G. L. Kuzmin appears in *Poshchechina obshchestvennomu vkusu* but in later books both Kuzmin and Dolinsky are credited as publishers. N. Khardzhiev has established that the book was to be collected by David Burliuk from the printers on 18 December 1912, see *NKh*: p. 16.

8. V. V. Kandinsky letter *Russkoe Slovo no. 102* 4 May 1913, Moscow. N. Khardzhiev has pointed out that Kandinsky and Burliuk had joint discussions during the six months leading up to the publication of *A Slap*, see *NKh*: p. 17.

9. '*Videt*' (*To See*) printed with woodcut vignette from the German edition (not included in original Russian publication in *A Slap*). See p. 5, V. V. Kandinsky: *Tekst khudozhnika*, Moscow, Otdel Izobrazitelnykh Iskusstv Narodnogo Kommissariata po Prosveshcheniyu, 1918. The book is described as a Russian translation of *Kandinsky's Album* published by Der Sturm, Berlin, 1914, but it also includes reproductions of several later works.

10. A. Kruchenykh: *15 let russkogo futurizma*, Moscow, 1928, pp. 58–9.

11. N. Khardzhiev and V. Trenin: *Poeticheskaya kultura Mayakovskogo*, Moscow, 1970.

12. Eli Eganbyuri: *Nataliya Goncharova – Mikhail Larionov*, Moscow, Myunster, 1913. In later years, Zdanevich admitted that his introductory article had been written in a hurry; however, the information it contains is valuable, especially after the recent publication of the precise date of the granting of Larionov's Diploma (see note 2 above).

13. The first edition of *Explodity* (*Vzorval*) contains a handwritten, lithographed endpage listing forthcoming books from the Moscow publishers, Kuzmin and Dolinsky, which includes *Vzorval* and *Bukh lesinnyi*. In later books, both are listed as having been published by *EUY*, the name which Kruchenykh chose for his own imprint.

14. Elena Guro died on 26 April 1913 according to the chronicle of literary events: 'Letopis literaturnykh sobytii 1908–1917' pp. 389–686, *Russkaya literatura kontsa XIX – nachala XXv.*, ed. B. A. Byalik, E. B. Tager, V. R. Shcherbina, Moscow, Nauka, 1972.

15. Reported in *Za 7 dnei no. 28 (122)*, pp. 605–6. See Charlotte Douglas 'Birth of a "Royal Infant": Malevich and "Victory over the Sun"' *Art in America*, March/April 1974, no. 2, pp. 45–51.

16. The poster was reproduced by Benedikt Livshits; see *The One and a Half-Eyed Archer*, trans. John E. Bowlt, Mass., Oriental Research Partners, 1977, p. 146, and translation Appendix 1, p. 248.

17. The poster is reproduced by Andrei B. Nakov: *Malevitch Écrits*, Paris, Champ Libre, 1975, p. 35.

18. The catalogue of this Union of Youth exhibition is reproduced in full in Valentine Marcadé: *L'Art Pictural Russe* (op. cit.) but Mme. Marcadé was unable to correct the mistake in dating before her book was published, so the exhibition is misleadingly printed on p. 319 (see further, p. 30 of this book and note 11 above).

19. V. Kamensky: *The Mud Hut (Zemlyanka)*, see *VM*: pp. 29–32.

20. I. Zdanevich and M. Larionov: 'Pochemu my raskrashivaemsya', in *Argus* (Christmas number), St Petersburg, 1913, pp. 114–18. For English translation with photographs of the original, see *JB*: pp. 79–83.

21. See Benedikt Livshits: 'My i zapad' *Polutoraglazyi strelets*, Leningrad, 1933: in English, chapter 7, 'We and the West', in *The One and a Half-Eyed Archer*, trans. John E. Bowlt, op. cit. Another version is given by Vahan D. Barooshian: *Russian Cubo-Futurism 1910–30*, The Hague/Paris, Mouton, 1974, pp. 148–52.

22. F. T. Marinetti: *Zang Tumb Tuum. Adrianopoli-ottobre 1912 – parole in libertà*, Milan, 1914, Edizioni futuriste di 'Poesia'. In *Lacerba*, advertised as '*di prossima pubblicazione*' among advertisements in *Anno II no. 2*, 15 January 1914, and in *Anno II no. 5*, 1 March 1914, p. 80: '*e uscito F. T. Marinetti Zang Tumb Tuum*'. This is the number of *Lacerba* following that in which Marinetti's Russian lecture tour is mentioned.

23. See Herman Berninger and Jean Cartier: *Jean Pougny (Ivan Puni) Catalogue de l'Oeuvre, Vol 1, Les années d'avant-garde. Russie-Berlin 1910–1923* (with many useful photographs of exhibition catalogues, translations of reviews, etc.)

24. 'Igor Severyanin' was the name used by Igor Vasilevich Lotarev; see *VM*: pp. 62–6 and his whole chapter on Ego-futurism.

25. *Knizhnaya letopis* is the Russian weekly bibliography which provides a record of dates for publications of all kinds. Judging by reviews chronicled in *Russkaya literatura 1908–17* op. cit., the entries in *Kn.l.* provide accurate dating, though writers and artists involved would have seen the books after printing and before sending them to the censor. See listing on pp. 125–7 of this book.

26. V. Shershenevich: *Futurism without a Mask* (*Futurizm bez maski*), Moscow, 'Iskusstvo', 1913 (*Kn.l.* no. 30704, 12–19 November).

27. See Andrei B. Nakov; *Alexandra Exter*, exhibition cat., Galerie Jean Chauvelin, Paris, 1972.

28. V. Kamensky: *Tango with Cows* (*Tango s korovami*), ill. D. Burliuk and V. Kamensky, and

A. Kravtsov: *The Naked One among the Clad* (*Nagoi sredi odetykh*), both Moscow, 1914. See chapter 4 below.

29. Both artists' works arrived late for the exhibition and were only included in the second edition of the catalogue.

30. See *Lacerba Anno II no. 8*, 15 April 1914, p. 143.

31. See Troels Andersen: *Malevich*, Stedelijk Museum Amsterdam, 1970, p. 9 for reproduction of photograph from *Ogonek*, (St Petersburg), 13 April 1914, showing Malevich's paintings installed in Paris.

32. Galerie Paul Guillaume, 17–30 June 1914; catalogue foreword written by Guillaume Apollinaire.

33. See *Lacerba Anno II no. 13*, 1 July 1914, p. 207.

34. See *Lacerba Anno III no. 15*, 10 April 1915, 'La venere del soldato', p. 125.

35. *VM*: pp. 277–83.

36. El Lissitzky 'Our book – 1926' abridged from *Gutenberg-Jahrbuch*, Mainz, 1926–7, quoted in English: Sophie Lissitzky-Küppers: *El Lissitzky – Life, letters and texts*, London, Thames and Hudson, 1968, pp. 357–8.

37. Konstantin Bolshakov: *The Spent Sun – second book of poems 1913–16* (*Solntse na izlete: vtoraya kniga stikhov 1913–16*). The title has previously been translated 'Sun in Decline' but the connection of '*na izlete*' with a 'spent bullet' fits the plight of the sun after 'Victory over the Sun'. Bolshakov's first book of poems, *Le Futur*, had been printed in 1913 but confiscated by the censor.

38. I. A. Aksenov: *Weak Foundations* (*Neuvazhitelnye osnovaniya*), Moscow, Centrifuge, 1916. Twenty-two poems with two full-page etchings by A. Ekster, numbered edition of two hundred copies (British Library no. 102). Aksenov is listed among contributors for the *First Journal of Russian Futurists 1–2* (*Pervyi zhurnal russkikh futuristov 1–2*). He published a monograph on Picasso: *Pikasso i okrestnosti*, Moscow, 1916 (cover design by A. Ekster), which is well illustrated with photographic reproductions.

39. K. Malevich: *From Cubism and Futurism to Suprematism: New Painterly Realism* (*Ot kubizma i futurizma k suprematizmu; novyi zhivopisnyi realizm*), 3rd printing, Moscow, 1916. English version: *K. S. Malevich Essays on Art 1915–33 Vol 1*, ed. Troels Andersen, translated by Xenia Glowacki-Prus and Arnold McMillin, London, Rapp & Whiting, André Deutsch, 1969, pp. 19–41.

40. K. Malevich: *From cubism to suprematism: new painterly realism* (*Ot kubizma k suprematizmu: novyi zhivopisnyi realizm*), Petrograd, Zhuravl,

1915. French version: *Écrits I. K Malévitch. De Cézanne au Suprématisme*, présentation de Jean-Claude Marcadé, Lausanne, L'Age d'Homme, 1974, pp. 35–43.

41. Installation photograph reproduced in *From Surface to Space, Russia 1916–24*, exhibition cat., Galerie Gmurzynska, Cologne, 1974, p. 41.

42. A. Kruchenykh: *Universal War* (*Vselenskaya voina*). Rozanova's collages are reproduced in *Tatlin's Dream, Russian Suprematist and Constructivist Art 1910–23*, exhibition cat., Fischer Fine Art, London, 1973–4, pp. 50–2.

3: THEATRE

1. *JB*: p. 13.

2. Oliver M. Sayler: *The Russian Theatre*, N.Y., Brentano's, 1922. See especially Chapter XIV, 'Yevreynoff and Monodrama', in which Saylor gives an English version of a large part of Evreinov's introduction to his monodrama, pp. 221–44.

3. *Studiya impressionistov*, p. 52.

4. Useful information on this theatre can be found in *Meyerhold on Theatre*, trans. and ed. with a critical commentary by Edward Braun, London, Methuen, 1969.

5. *Vvedenie v monodramu*, St Petersburg, N. I. Butkovskoi, 1909.

6. In the Russian title '*V kulisakh dushi*' Evreinov employs the French word *coulisse* which would more closely be translated 'In the slips of the soul' than 'In the Greenroom of the soul'.

7. *Studiya impressionistov*, p. 53.

8. idem, p. 56.

9. idem, colour plate opp. p. 112.

10. idem, printed underneath plate opp. p. 96. See colour plate 14 of this book.

11. A 'drawing from nature at the time of the spectacle Vladimir Mayakovsky – A Tragedy' by S. Zhivotovsky is reproduced in *Dekorativnoe iskusstvo SSSR 6/187*, 1973, p. 40.

12. *Studiya impressionistov*, p. 56.

13. '*Vladimir Mayakovsky*' – *Tragediya*, Moscow, 1914, p. 18.

14. idem, pp. 35–8.

15. For descriptions of this production see Constantin Stanislavsky: *My Life in Art*, trans. by J. J. Robins, London, Penguin, 1967, chap. 54, 'Isadora Duncan and Gordon Craig', and also Denis Bablet: *Edward Gordon Craig*, London, Heinemann, 1966.

16. Marussia Burliuk: 'Mayakovsky and the theatre (1911 Dec)', *Color and Rhyme no. 31* (*1955*), N.Y., p. 16.

17. idem.

18. Quoted in Wictor Woroszylski: *The Life of Mayakovsky*, trans. from the Polish by Boleslaw

Taborski, London, Gollancz, 1972, p. 77. (Russian source L. Zheverzheev 'Vospominaniya' in *Mayakovskomu*, Leningrad, 1940).

19. See chapter 2, note 16.

20. See chapter 2, note 15.

21. Klaus Lankheit: *The Blaue Reiter Almanac: The Documents of 20th-century Art*, London, Thames and Hudson, 1974, note 5, pp. 194–5.

22. idem, p. 210.

23. idem, p. 213.

24. See *Rudolf Steiner 1861–1925*, Dornach, The Goetheanum School of Spiritual Science, 1964, pp. 25–6.

25. See *Pobeda nad solntsem*, Viktor Khlebnikov, *prolog*.

26. Benedikt Livshits: *Polutoraglazyi strelets*, Leningrad, 1933, p. 187. (The heading for the first two lines of the prologue is *chernotvorskiya vestuchki* which is almost untranslatable.)

27. *Studiya impressionistov*, p. 53.

28. Klaus Lankheit: *The Blaue Reiter Almanac*, op. cit., following p. 243.

29. idem, L. Sabaneiev 'Scriabin's ''Prometheus''', pp. 127–40.

30. Benedikt Livshits, op.cit., p. 187.

31. The production named by Livshits was Prokofiev's 'Love of Three Oranges', designed by Isaak Rabinovich in 1928. The transformation of Vera Komissarzhevskaya's theatre by Niezlobin, who introduced 'American attractions' into the garden next door which was enlarged and with the 'indoor theatre received the American name, Luna Park', is described by K. Tomashevsky who acted in 'Victory over the Sun' and 'Vladimir Mayakovsky – A Tragedy' – see 'Vladimir Mayakovsky' *Teatr no. 4*, 1938, translated in *TDR/The Drama Review Vol. 15 no. 4 (T–52)*, Fall, 1971, p. 96.

32. Some of Malevich's costume designs for 'Victory over the Sun' were reproduced in colour in *Projekt 5 61/1967*, (Warsaw), p. 21, in an article by Szymon Bojko: 'Malevich stage-designer'.

33. Benedikt Livshits: *Polutoraglazyi strelets*, op. cít., p. 188.

34. *Pobeda nad solntsem* is reproduced in a dual language edition: *La Victoire sur le Soleil*, trans. with notes and postscript by V. and J.-C. Marcadé in *Théâtre Années Vingt* series, Lausanne, L'Age d'Homme, 1976. English trans. 'Victory over the Sun', Ewa Bartos and Victoria Nes Kirby in *TDR/The Drama Review Vol. 15, no. 4 (T–52)*, Fall, 1971, pp. 107–24.

35. A. Kruchenykh: 'Novye puti slova (yazyk budushchego smert simvolizmu)' *Troe*, St Petersburg, Zhuravl, 1913, pp. 22–41, reproduced in Vladimir Markov: *Manifesty i programmy russkikh futuristov, Slavische Propyläen Band 27*, Munich, Wilhelm Fink, 1967,

pp. 64–72.

36. *TDR/The Drama Review (T-52)*, op. cit, p. 119.

37. Quoted from *TDR/The Drama Review (T-52)*, op. cit., pp. 101–4, where Matyushin's article 'Futurism in St Petersburg – Performances on the 2nd, 3rd, 4th and 5th December 1913' is translated in full. Russian source: *Pervyi zhurnal russkikh futuristov 1–2 (First Journal of Russian futurists 1–2)*.

38. From '*Khudozhnik Aristarkh Lentulov*', memoirs of M. Lentulov, Moscow, 1969, pp. 28–9, quoted in Russian by L. Zhadova, 'Teatr Mayakovskogo. Stranitsy istorii.' *Dekorativnoe Iskusstvo SSSR 6/187*, 1963, p. 41. In French '''*Des Commencements sans fins*'' sur le théâtre futuriste russe' L. Jadova, *Europe, revue littéraire mensuelle 53 année – No 552* Paris, April 1975, pp. 128–9.

39. This quotation from Edward Braun: *Meyerhold on Theatre*, op. cit., p. 191. See also the two articles by Larissa Zhadova cited in previous note.

40. Benedikt Livshits: *The One and a Half-Eyed Archer*, trans. by John E. Bowlt, op. cit., p. 164.

41. See chapter 2, note 39.

42. See chapter 2, note 18.

43. Reproduced *La Victoire sur le Soleil, édition bilangue*, op. cit., p. 62.

44. 27 May 1915, Pushkin House archive; cited in Russian 'K. S. Malevich: pisma k M. V. Matyushinu' published by E. F. Kovtun in *Ezhegodnik rukopisnogo otdela Pushkinskogo doma na 1974 god*, Leningrad, Nauka 1976, pp. 177–95. Cited in English translation, E. F. Kovtun, 'The Beginning of Suprematism', *From Surface to Space, Russia 1916–24*, exhibition cat., Galerie Gmurzynska, Cologne, 1974, pp. 32–47.

45. It is not without significance that Benedikt Livshits described himself as a Freudian at that time.

46. *TDR/The Drama Review (T-52)*, op. cit., p. 115.

47. See chapter 2, note 17.

48. Some of these drawings are reproduced by Miroslav Lamač: 'Malevič a jeho okruh' *Vytvarné Umení 8/9*, 1967, (Prague), pp. 373–83.

49. An account of Zdanevich's years in France can be found in *La rencontre Iliazd-Picasso Hommage à Iliazd*, exhibition cat., Musée d'Art Moderne de la Ville de Paris, 1976. For the preceding years in Tiflis see *VM*: pp. 350–8.

50. Cesare G. De Michelis: *Il futurismo Italiano in Russia 1909–29, temi i problemi*, Bari, De Donato, 1973. See p. 270, ref. Eshmer Valdor (Recensione a '*Roi Bombance*' di Marinetti) in *Vesy IX*, 1906.

51. Note especially the hand-written,

illustrated text, *Ubu Roi*, published by Editions Mercure de France in 1897.

52. *TDR/The Drama Review* (*T-52*), op. cit., p. 109.

53. See *VM*: pp. 354–5. I confess that I have relied entirely on Professor Markov's full description of the text which I find undecipherable!

54. Note 3 p. 154 '"Des Commencements sans fins" sur le théâtre futuriste russe' Larissa Jadova *Europe*, April 1975, op. cit.

55. idem, p. 126.

56. V. Mayakovsky: *Dlya golosa*, Berlin, Gosudarstvennoe izdatelstvo RSFSR, 1923.

57. See Edward Braun: *Meyerhold on Theatre*, op. cit., p. 188–9.

4: GRAPHIC DESIGN

1. See especially William Blake: *Songs of Innocence*, 1789, and *Songs of Experience*, 1794. For reproductions and discussion see Martin Butlin: *William Blake*, exhibition cat., Tate Gallery, London, 1978, pp. 44–5 and 48–50.

2. See *Gore: skazka*, ill. E. E. Lissner, Moscow, Goznak, 1973, and Aleksandr Pushkin: *The Tale of Tsar Saltan*, ill. I. Bililbin, 1905, trans. Louis Zellikoff, Moscow, Progress, n.d.

3. T. E. Griffits: *The Rudiments of Lithography*, London, Faber and Faber, 1956.

4. See John E. Bowlt: 'Nikolai Ryabushinsky Playboy of the Eastern World', *Apollo* (*The Silver Age of Russian Art*) (London) December 1973, pp. 486–93.

5. Tipped in to the British Library copy of A. Kruchenykh, *The Word as Such* (*Slovo kak takovoe*) is the three-page leaflet *Declaration of the Word as Such* (*Deklaratsiya slova, kak takovogo*) which opens with an article signed A. Kruchenykh 19 April with a footnote dating *A Trap for Judges* (*Sadok sudei*) to 1908. The 'Foundation manifesto of Italian futurism' by F. T. Marinetti was published simultaneously in France and Italy, 20 February 1909.

6. See chapter two, note 28.

7. Modern reprints of these postcards were on sale at the Victoria and Albert Museum, London during the exhibition 'Hommage to Kokoschka – Prints and Drawings from the collection of Reinhold, Count Bethusy-Huc', 1976.

8. This correspondence quoted by N. Khardzhiev: 'Mayakovsky i zhivopis' *Mayakovsky: materialy i issledovaniya*, Moscow, Nauka, 1940, p. 358, note 1: 1 March 1911 V. Kandinsky wrote to N. Goncharova: '. . . He (Larionov) wrote only casually to me about his publication and so I would like to know what it is . . . And in what consists this "Donkey's Tail"' (unpublished letter).

9. See postcards by M. Larionov, Print-room, Victoria and Albert Museum, London.

10. *Der Sturm no. 22*, 28 July 1910, p. 174: 'Head of Walden'; *no. 27* 1 September 1910: 'Head of Paul Scheerbart; *no. 39* 24 November 1910: cover design 'Ausruhende Tänzerin', 5 January 1911: 'Vorüber'; *no. 106* April 1912: cover illustration.

11. For extracts from this catalogue see Tatiana Loguine: *Gontcharova et Larionov, cinquante ans à Saint Germain-des-Prés*, Paris, Klincksieck, 1971, pp. 33–7.

12. See Yury Ovsyannikov: *Lubok – The Lubok* (English trans. Arthur Shkarovsky-Raffe) Moscow, Sovetsky khudozhnik, 1968.

13. *Lacerba Anno III no. 15*, 10 April, 1915.

14. G. Apollinaire, 'Zone', first published in *Les Soirées de Paris*, December 1912.

15. The exact dating of *La Prose du Transsibérien et de la Petite Jehanne de France* is difficult to establish, though the evidence points to October 1913 as the date of publication. (See Marc Poupon: 'Apollinaire et Cendrars', *Archives des lettres Modernes 103*, Paris, 1969, esp. notes and appendix.) In November 1913 a copy was exhibited in Berlin – see *Der Sturm no. 184*, 5 November 1913, p. 127, and see *Apollon*, January/February 1914, article on lecture by A. Smirnov in St Petersburg which included a showing of the book.

16. Vladimir Tatlin provided a single lithograph for *Worldbackwards* (*Mirskontsa*); two of his drawings were printed in *The Service-book of the Three* (*Trebnik troikh*), April 1913; Tatlin was away from Russia on a visit to Europe during the summer of 1913 and contributed to no other Russian futurist books.

17. There are several examples in the Print room, Victoria and Albert Museum, London.

18. The copy in the British Library collection is no. 1 of an edition of five hundred. It is signed by Sergei Bobrov and Nataliya Goncharova. The article on book design is on pp. 153–6.

19. V. Parkin, 'Oslinyi khvost i mishen', *Oslinyi khvost i mishen*, pp. 51–82.

20. Reproduced in Troels Andersen: *Malevich*, Stedelijk Museum Amsterdam, 1970, p. 101, cat. nos. 74, 75, collection Kupferstichkabinett der oeffentlichen Kunstsammlung, Kunstmuseum, Basel.

21. Reproduced in *From Surface to Space, Russia 1916–24*, exhibition cat., Galerie Gmurzynska, Cologne, 1974, p. 35.

22. *NKh*: p. 96.

23. *NKh*:, p. 95.

24. Some pages from the book are reproduced in *NKh* following p. 127.

25. See an advertisement page at the back of *The Word as Such* (*Slovo kak takovoe*) – 'Printed

and shortly to be put on sale one hundred copies of *A Duck's Nest* (*Utinoe gnezdyshko*) A. Kruchenykh drawings and painting O. Rozanova.' (Although the book had been advertised in the summer, it was not registered in *Knizhnaya letopis* until the end of December 1913.)

26. See chapter one, note 14.

27. There may also be a deliberately futurist pun in the fact that Kamensky's own name contains the ordinary Russian word for 'a stone' (*kamen*), a traditional material of which ferro-concrete could be seen as a modern, man-made equivalent.

28. Kamensky's poem in the shape of a fez is reproduced by Krystyna Pomorska: *Russian Formalist Theory and its Poetic Ambience*, The Hague/Paris, Mouton, 1968, p. 109. The source is unclear, but the idea is extremely close to Apollinaire.

29. See chapter two, note 36.

30. The Russian word for 'book' is '*kniga*', the substitution of a 'g' for the 'k' suggests a pun on the words for 'book' and 'nit' (*kniga – gnida*) see *VM*: p. 334. The cover and some pages are reproduced as entry 134 in the cat. *Constructivism and Futurism: Russian and other. Ex Libris 6*, New York, T. J. Art Inc., 1977.

31. See chapter two, note 42.

5: RUSSIAN FUTURIST BOOKS AND THE DEVELOPMENT OF AVANT-GARDE PAINTING

1. Reproduced in colour by Will Grohmann: *Vasily Kandinsky, Life and Work*, N.Y./London, Abrams, 1959, p. 101.

2. M. Larionov: 'Luchistskaya zhivopis' *Oslinyi khvost i mishen* pp. 83–124, quoted in English in *JB*: pp. 93–100. These extracts pp. 96, 98, 93.

3. Umberto Boccioni, Carlo Carrà, Luigi Russolo, Giacomo Balla, Gino Severini: 'Futurist Painting: Technical Manifesto' (leaflet), Milan, Poesia, 11 April 1910. (English version in *Futurist Manifestos*, ed. Umbro Apollonio, London, Thames and Hudson, 1973, pp. 27–31.) It was this manifesto which was translated into Russian and printed in the second journal of the *Union of Youth* (*Soyuz molodezhi 2*) June 1912.

4. See *NKh*: p. 39. N. Khardzhiev quotes a letter of 20 September 1912 from L. Zheverzheev to Larionov thanking him for his article about rayism. Two rayist canvases, 'Portrait of a fool' and 'Rayist sausage and mackerel' – reproduced in *Donkey's Tail and Target* (*Oslinyi khvost i mishen*) and *Rayism* (*Luchizm*) – were shown by Larionov at the Union of Youth exhibition

December 1912–January 1913. See chapter two, note 18 and refs.

5. I am indebted for this interpretation, which I have subsequently found totally convincing, to Rory Doepel. His work on the imagery of Juan Miro's paintings of the 1920s suggested these connections.

6. See Benedikt Livshits: *The One and a Half-Eyed Archer*, trans. John E. Bowlt, p. 57.

7. At his death, part of Larionov's library was acquired by the British Art Library, Victoria and Albert Museum, London.

8. Study collection, Museum of Modern Art, N.Y., ref. *M. Larionov 40.36*.

9. See note 2.

10. idem.

11. See A. E. Elsen: *Rodin*, N.Y., Museum of Modern Art, 1963, pp. 118–19.

12. V. Markov: 'Printsipy novogo iskusstva' *Soyuz molodezhi I*, pp. 5–14, and *Soyuz molodezhi 2*, pp. 5–18, translated in *JB*: pp. 25–38 (with omissions).

13. Nikolai Kulbin: 'Svobodnoe iskusstvo, kak osnova zhizni. Garmoniya i dissonans (O zhizni, smerti i prochem)' *Impressionists' Studio* (*Studiya impressionistov*), pp. 3–14. Extracts in *JB*: pp. 13–17; this quote, p. 15.

14. The article 'Kubizm' was signed N(ikolai) Burliuk but all sources are agreed that it, and the companion theoretical article 'Faktura', were written by David Burliuk and not by his younger brother, the poet. David Burliuk: 'Cubism (Surface-plane)', translated in *JB*: pp. 70–77.

15. N. Khardzhiev: 'Mayakovsky i zhivopis' *Mayakovsky: materialy i issledovaniya*, Moscow, Nauka, 1940, p. 361.

16. M. Larionov's 'Blue rayism' is reproduced in Camilla Gray: *The Great Experiment in Russian Art 1863–1922*, London, Thames and Hudson, 1962, plate IX opp. p. 124. The initials 'M L' are at the bottom left-hand corner, but when turned once to the right, so they are on the right, the painting is seen closely to resemble the contemporary photograph of 'Portrait of a fool' reproduced in *Donkey's Tail and Target* (*Oslinyi khvost i mishen*).

17. The manifesto is reproduced in V. Markov: *Manifesty i programmy russkikh futuristov*, Slavische Propyläen Band 27, Munich, Fink, 1967, pp. 50–51 and translated in *VM* pp. 45–6.

18. B. Livshits: 'Osvobozhdenie slova' *Dokhlaya luna*, reprinted in V. Markov: *Manifesty i programmy*, op. cit., pp. 73–7. English quotation from *VM*: p. 120.

19. O. Rozanova: 'Osnovy novogo tvorchestva i prichiny ego neponimaniya' *Soyuz molodezhi 3*, pp. 14–22. Translated in *JB*: pp. 103–10. Quoted here: pp. 103, 106, 108.

20. Reproduced in Benedikt Livshits: *The One*

and a Half-Eyed Archer, trans. John E. Bowlt, op. cit., p. 47: David Burliuk: 'Landscape from four points of view 1911'.

21. See note 3 above.

22. Among the Hylaeans interest in children's art was strong; in 1914 Kruchenykh published *Actual stories and drawings of children* (*Sobstvennye razskazy i risunki detei*), St Petersburg, EUY; the joint author (with Kruchenykh) of *Piglets* (*Porosyata*), who was named as Zina V, was described as a twelve-year old.

23. See Susan P. Compton: 'Malevich's Suprematism – the Higher intuition', *The Burlington Magazine*, no. 881, Vol. CXVIII, August 1976, for a slightly different approach to this subject.

24. One of the coloured lithographs by N. Goncharova in *Gardeners over the Vines* (*Vertogradari nad lozami*) represents 'kamennye baby'. Photographs of a number of these sculptures are included in S. I. Vainshtein *Istoriya narodnogo iskusstva Tuvy*, Moscow, Nauka, 1974, pp. 68–9.

25. P. D. Uspensky: *Tertium Organum*, St Petersburg, 1911.

26. Albert Gleizes, Jean Metzinger: *Du Cubisme*, Paris, Eugène Figuière et Cie, 27 December 1912.

27. Esprit Pascal Jouffret: *Traité élémentaire de géométrie à quatre dimensions et introduction à la géométrie à 'n' dimensions*, Paris, 1903.

28. See Lynda Dalrymple Henderson: 'The Fourth dimension and non-Euclidian Geometry Reinterpreted', *The Art Quarterly*, (Winter 1971), pp. 410–33; Susan Compton: 'Malevich and the Fourth Dimension', *Studio International*, Vol. 187 no. 965, April 1974 (n.b. diagram 3, lower figure inverted by the printer), and Lynda Dalrymple Henderson: 'The Merging of Time and Space: "The Fourth Dimension" in Russia from Ouspensky to Malevich', *The Structurist* (*Space/Time*), no. 15/16, 1975/6, Saskatoon, Canada, pp. 97–108.

29. C. Howard Hinton: *The Fourth Dimension*, N.Y./London, 1904.

30. M. Matyushin: 'An artist's creative path' (Manuscript), 1934, p. 140. SMIL Matyushin Archive. Quoted in English, Alla Povelikhina: 'Matyushin's spatial system', *The Isms of Art in Russia 1907–30*, exhibition cat., Galerie Gmurzynska, Cologne, 1977, pp. 27–41.

31. *The Three* (*Troe*) quoted in English by Alla Povelikhina as above. (An abridged version of Alla Povelikhina's important article was published in *The Structurist* (*Space/Time*), op. cit., p. 64.)

32. Reprinted in V. Markov: *Manifesty i programmy* op. cit., pp. 65–73; this quote p. 66. The original passage can be found in English in

P. D. Uspensky: *Tertium Organum – The Third canon of thought. A key to the enigmas of the world*, trans. Nicholas Bessarabov and Claude Bragdon, 2nd edition (chapters XI and XV not included in the original 1911 edition), London, Routledge and Kegan Paul, 1973, p. 73.

33. P. D. Uspensky *Tertium Organum*, idem, p. 301.

34. Two of this series are reproduced by Troels Andersen: *Malevich*, Stedelijk Museum Amsterdam, 1970, pp. 9 and 24.

35. I am grateful to Valya Coe for her help in this interpretation.

36. See chapter 1, note 14.

37. The pages in *Explodity* (*Vzorval*) are unnumbered: in the British Library copy of the first edition this announcement was made on leaf 27.

38. A. Kruchenykh informed N. Khardzhiev of the authorship of this drawing; see *NKh*: p. 93.

39. See N. Khardzhiev: 'Mayakovsky i zhivopis', op. cit., p. 359.

40. See Troels Andersen: *Malevich*, op. cit., Cat. entry 31, entitled 'The Orthodox' from the title of the related drawing in *The Non-Objective World*. A photograph of the painting was reproduced in *Ogonek* in a review of the Union of Youth exhibition 1911–12 and the title was given as 'Portrait of Ivan Klyunkov'; no painting entitled 'The Orthodox' was included in the catalogue of that exhibition.

41. Daniil Kharms-Shardam: 'On the death of Kazimir Malevich' '*Na smert Kazimira Malevicha*', 17 May 1935. Manuscript reproduced with translation in Troels Andersen: *Malevich*, op. cit. p. 16.

42. See note 3 above.

43. Although none of Fernand Léger's paintings entitled '*Contrastes des formes*' were exhibited in Russia, a photograph of his '*Dynamisme obtenu par contrastes de blancs et noirs et complémentaires de lignes (dessin rehaussé)*' was reproduced in *Montjoie*, no. 9–10, 14–29 June 1913, p. 9, together with the text of the second part of a lecture which Léger had given at the Academie Vassiliev in Paris on 5 May 1913.

44. *The Three* (*Troe*), p. 82.

45. 'Victory over the Sun', trans. Ewa Bartos and Victoria Nes Kirby, *TDR/The Drama Review* Vol. 15 no. 4 (T-52), Fall 1971, p. 119.

46. See chapter two, note 20.

47. Benedikt Livshits: *The One and a Half-Eyed Archer*, trans. John E. Bowlt, op. cit., p. 163; also reproduced in Troels Andersen: *Malevich*, op. cit., p. 24.

48. *NKh*: p. 95.

49. *Malevich: Suprematism. 34 Drawings*, facsimile reprint with trans. by Thomas H. Winner, London, Gordon Fraser, 1974.

50. See chapter 4, p. 79.

51. See *VM*: p. 80.

52. K. Malevich: *Ot kubizma k suprematizmu:novyi zhivopisnyi realizm*, Petrograd, Zhuravl, 1915, on sale at the Zero-ten Exhibition in December. Author's trans. from the French: *Du cubisme au suprématisme – le nouveau réalisme pictural* in *K. Malévitch: De Cézanne au suprématisme*, ed. Jean-Claude et Valentine Marcadé, Lausanne, L'Age d'Homme, pp. 37–43; this quote p. 43.

53. See chapter 2, note 42.

54. *See NKh*: p. 94.

55. See chapter 4, p. 79.

56. El Lissitzky: *Of Two Squares (Pro dva kvadrata)*, Berlin, 1922, reprinted in facsimile in Sophie Lissitzky-Küppers: *El Lissitzky. Life, letters and text*, London, Thames and Hudson, 1968, colour plates 80–91.

57. 'Victory over the Sun', *TDR/The Drama Review (T-52)*, op. cit., p. 124.

A list of futurist and related books arranged
chronologically in order of appearance in *Knizhnaya letopis'*.
Items marked * are not held by the British Library.

Kn.l. = *Knizhnaya letopis'*.

СТУДИЯ ИМПРЕССИОНИСТОВ
(The Impressionists' Studio)
ed. N. Kul'bin; ill. N. Kul'bin
(et al.) SPb.: N.I. Butkovskoi,
1910. 127p. 27.5 x 20cm. 2,000
copies.
(Kn.1.no.7762. 24-31 March)

САДОК СУДЕЙ (A Trap for Judges)
V. Kamensky (et al.) (SPb.:
Zhuravl', 1910.) 131 leaves.
ill. 12.2 x 11.3cm. 300 copies.
(Kn.1.no.11495. 11-18 May)

ОБЩЕСТВО ХУДОЖНИКОВ "СОЮЗ МОЛОДЕЖИ"*
(Society of Artists "Union of
Youth") no.1. April 1912. SPb.,
1912. ill. 24.2 x 16.5cm. 500
copies.
(Kn.1.no.12552. 1-8 May)

ОБЩЕСТВО ХУДОЖНИКОВ "СОЮЗ МОЛОДЕЖИ"*
(Society of Artists "Union of
Youth") no.2. June 1912. SPb.,
1912. ill. 24.2 x 16.5cm. 500
copies.
(Kn.1.no.16753. 19 June-2 July)

ИГРА В АДУ: поэма (A Game in Hell:
a poem)
A. Kruchenykh, V. Khlebnikov; ill.
N. Goncharova. M.(: G.L. Kuzmin &
S.D. Dolinsky, 1912). 14 leaves.
18.5 x 14.5cm. 300 copies.
(Kn.1.no.27432. 15-22 Oct.)

СТАРИННАЯ ЛЮБОВЬ (Old-Time Love)
A. Kruchenykh; ill. M. Larionov.
M.(: G.L. Kuzmin & S.D. Dolinsky,
1912). 13 leaves. 14.5 x 9.7cm
300 copies.
(Kn.1.no.27431. 15-22 Oct.)

МИРСКОНЦА (Worldbackwards)
A. Kruchenykh, V. Khlebnikov;
ill. N. Goncharova, M. Larionov,
V. Tatlin, I. Rogovin. M.(: G.L.
Kuzmin & S.D. Dolinsky, 1912).
(41) leaves, (3 blank). 18.6 x
15cm. 220 copies.
(Kn.1.no.33950. 10-17 Dec.)

ПОЩЕЧИНА ОБЩЕСТВЕННОМУ ВКУСУ
(A Slap in the Face of Public
Taste) D. & N. Burlyuk (et al.)
M: G.L. Kuzmin, (1912). 112p.
25.2 x 19cm. 600 copies.
(Kn.1.no.1776. 7-14 Jan. 1913)

ПУСТЫННИКИ: поэма (Hermits: a poem)
A. Kruchenykh; ill. N. Goncharova.
(M:) G.L. Kuzmin & S.D. Dolinsky,
(1913). (22)leaves. 19 x 14.5cm.
480 copies.
(Kn.1.no.3995. 28 Jan.-4 Feb.)

ПОЛУЖИВОЙ (Half-Alive)
A. Kruchenykh; ill. M. Larionov.
M: G.L. Kuzmin & S.D. Dolinsky,
(1913). (17) leaves. 18.2 x 14.7cm.
480 copies.
(Kn.1.no.5549. 18-25 Feb).

ПОМАДА (Pomade)
A. Kruchenykh; ill. M. Larionov.
M.: G.L. Kuzmin & S.D. Dolinsky,
(1913). (17) leaves. 15.2 x 10.9cm.
480 copies.
(Kn.1.no.5548. 18-25 Feb.)

САДОК СУДЕЙ II (A Trap for Judges 2)
(SPb.:) Zhuravl', (1913). 107p. ill.
19.6 x 17.3cm. 800 copies.
(Kn.1.no.6267. 25 Feb-4 March)

"СОЮЗ МОЛОДЕЖИ" при участии поэтов
"ГИЛЕЯ" ("Union of Youth" with the
participation of the "HYLEA" poets)
no.3. March 1913. ill. I. Shkol'nik,
O. Rozanova. SPb., 1913. 82p. 24 x
24cm. 1,000 copies.
(Kn.1.no.8787. 25 March-1 April)

ТРЕБНИК ТРОИХ (Service-Book of the
Three)
V. Khlebnikov, V. Mayakovsky, D. &
N. Burlyuk; ill. D, N. & V. Burlyuk,
V. Mayakovsky, N. Tatlin. M.: G.L.
Kuzmin & S.D. Dolinsky, 1913.
86p., (15) leaves of plates. 21 x
17.6cm. 1,100 copies.
(Kn.1.no.9413. 1-8 April)

ЛУЧИЗМ (Rayism)*
M. Larionov; ill. N. Goncharova,
M. Larionov. (M.: Ts. A. Myunster,
1913). 21p., (6) leaves of plates.
14.4 x 11.3cm. 1,000 copies.
(Kn.1.no.10313. 22-29 April)

БУХ ЛЕСИННЫЙ (A Forestly Rapid)
A. Kruchenykh, V. Khlebnikov;
ill. O. Rozanova, N. Kul'bin,
A. Kruchenykh. (SPb.:) EUY,
(1913). (22) leaves. 14.5 x
9.5cm. 400 copies.
(Kn.1.no.14412. 3-10 June)

ВЗОРВАЛЬ (Explodity)
A. Kruchenykh; ill. N. Kul'bin,
O. Rozanova, K. Malevich, N.
Goncharova. (Spb.: EUY, 1913).
(31) leaves. 17.7 x 12.2cm.
350 copies.
(Kn.1.no.14411. 3-10 June)

ВОЗРОПЩЕМ (Let's Grumble)
A. Kruchenykh; ill. K. Malevich,
O. Rozanova. (SPb.: EUY, 1913).
12p., (3) leaves of plates. 18.5
x 13.5cm. 1,000 copies.
(Kn.1.no.15182. 10-17 June)

ВЕРТОГРАДАРИ НАД ЛОЗАМИ
(Gardeners over the Vines)
S. Bobrov; ill. N. Goncharova.
M.: Lirika, 1913. 162p., (20)
leaves of plates. 18 x 11.7cm.
500 copies.
(Kn.1.no.18037. 15-23 July)

НАТАЛИЯ ГОНЧАРОВА. МИХАИЛ ЛАРИОНОВ*
(Nataliya Goncharova. Mikhail
Larionov)
Eli Eganbyuri. M.: Ts. A. Myunster,
1913. 39, xxiip., (54) leaves of
plates. ill. 28.2 x 21.5cm. 525
copies.
(Kn.1.no.19060. 23-30 July)

ОСЛИНЫЙ ХВОСТ И МИШЕНЬ
(Donkey's Tail and Target) M.:
Ts. A. Myunster, 1913. 151p.
28.7 x 23cm. 525 copies.
(Kn.1.no.18843. 23-30 July)

ПОРОСЯТА (Piglets)
Zina V., A. Kruchenykh. (SPb.:
EUY), 1913. 15p. 19.5 x 14.5cm.
550 copies.
(Kn.1.no.20675. 13-20 Aug.)

ТРОЕ (The Three)
V. Khlebnikov, A. Kruchenykh,
E. Guro; ill. K. Malevich. SPb.:
Zhuravl', (1913). 96p. 20 x 19cm.
500 copies.
(Kn.1.no.24569. 17-24 Sept.)

СЛОВО КАК ТАКОВОЕ (The Word as Such)
A. Kruchenykh, V. Khlebnikov; ill.
K. Malevich, O. Rozanova. (M.,
1913.) 15p., (1) leaf of plates.
22.2 x 17cm. 500 copies.
(Kn.1.no.27034. 15-22 Oct.)
Insert: Декларация слова, как
такового (Declaration of the Word
as Such)
A. Kruchenykh, N. Kul'bin. (SPb.,
1913). 3p. 21.5 x 15cm.

ЗАТЫЧКА (The Bung)
V. Khlebnikov, D., V. & N. Burlyuk;
ill. V. Burlyuk. M.: "Lit Ko."
Futuristov "Gileya". (1913). 13p.,
(4) leaves of plates. 23.3 x 18cm.
450 copies.
(Kn.1.no.27804. 22-29 Oct.)

НЕО-ПРИМИТИВИЗМ (Neo-Primitivism)
A. Shevchenko. M., 1913. 31p.,
(14) leaves of plates. ill. 22.4
x 17.3cm. 1,000 copies.
(Kn.1.no.31348. 19-26 Nov.)

ЧОРТ И РЕЧЕТВОРЦЫ (The Devil and
the Wordmakers)
A. Kruchenykh; (cover) ill. O.
Rozanova. (SPb.: EUY, 1913).
16p. 22.5 x 16.7cm. 1,000 copies.
(Kn.1.no.31792. 26 Nov.-3 Dec.)

ВЗОРВАЛЬ (Explodity)
A. Kruchenykh; ill. N. Kul'bin,
O. Rozanova, K. Malevich, N.
Goncharova. (Spb.: EUY, 1913).
2nd enl. ed. (29) leaves. 18.1 x
12.7cm. 450 copies.
(Kn.1.no.192. 20 Dec. 1913-1 Jan
1914).

ПОБЕДА НАД СОЛНЦЕМ: опера (Victory
over the Sun: an opera)
A. Kruchenykh; music M. Matyushin;
(cover) ill. K. Malevich, D. Burlyuk.
(SPb.: EUY, 1913). 23p. 24 x 17cm.
1,000 copies.
(Kn.1.no.193. 20 Dec. 1913-1 Jan.
1914)

РЯВ! ПЕРЧАТКИ! (Roar! Gauntlets!)
V. Khlebnikov; ill. D. Burlyuk,
K. Malevich. (M.:) EUY, (1914).
29p. 24.5 x 17.1cm. 1,000 copies.
(Kn.1.no.400. 20 Dec. 1913-1 Jan.
1914)

УТИНОЕ ГНЕЗДЫШКО... ДУРНЫХ СЛОВ*
(A Duck's Nest... of Bad Words)
A. Kruchenykh; ill. O. Rozanova.
(SPb.: EUY), 1913. (24) leaves.
17.5 x 12cm. 500 copies.
(Kn.1.no.194. 20 Dec. 1913-1 Jan.
1914).

ПРИНЦИПЫ КУБИЗМА И ДРУГИХ СОВРЕМ-
ЕННЫХ ТЕЧЕНИЙ В ЖИВОПИСИ...
(Principles of Cubism...)
A. Shevchenko. M.: Izd. A. Shev-
chenko, 1913. 24 leaves. 16.4 x
12.4cm.
(Not in Kn.1.)

LE FUTUR*
K. Bol'shakov; ill. N. Goncharova,
M. Larionov. (M.?) (1913). (17)
leaves. 19.9 x 15.5cm.
(Not in Kn.1. Confiscated by
censor)

ДОХЛАЯ ЛУНА (The Croaked Moon)
D., V. & N. Burlyuk (et al.); ill.
V. & D. Burlyuk. Autumn 1913. M.:
"Lit. Ko." Futuristov "Gileya",
1913. 119p. (18) leaves of plates.
19.5 x 15.2cm. 1,000 copies.
(kn.1.no.657. 1-8 Jan. 1914)

ФУТУРИСТЫ: РЫКАЮЩИЙ ПАРНАС
(Futurists: Roaring Parnassus)
D. Burlyuk (et al.); ill. D.
Burlyuk (et al.) (SPb.: Zhuravl',
1914) 119p. 21.3 x 17cm. 1,000
copies.
(Kn.1.no.4065. 5-12 Feb.)

ИГРА В АДУ (A Game in Hell)
A. Kruchenykh, V. Khlebnikov,
ill. O. Rozanova, K. Malevich
(cover) 2nd enl. ed. (M.: G.
L. Kuzmin & S.D. Dolinsky, 1914)
(40) leaves. 19 x 14cm. 800
copies.
(Kn.1.no.4452. 12-19 Feb.)

ТЭ ЛИ ЛЭ (Te li le)
A. Kruchenykh, V. Khlebnikov.
ill. O. Rozanova, N. Kul'bin.
SPb., 1914. (14) leaves. 23 x
17cm. 50 copies.
(Kn.1.no.4453. 12-19 Feb.)

МОЛОКО КОБЫЛИЦ (The Milk of Mares)
V. Khlebnikov (et al.); ill. A.
Ekster, D. & V. Burlyuk. M.:
"Lit. Ko." Futuristov "Gileya",
1914. 89p., (12) leaves of plates.
19.3 x 12.5cm. 400 copies.
(Kn.1.no.5426. 19-26 Feb.)

НАГОЙ СРЕДИ ОДЕТЫХ*
(The Naked One among the Clad)
V. Kamensky, A. Kravtsov; ill.
V. Kamensky. M., 1914. (28)
leaves. 19.7 x 19.7cm. 300
copies.
(Kn.1.no.5074. 19-26 Feb.)

ИЗБОРНИК СТИХОВ... 1907-1914
(Selection of Poems... 1907-1914)
V. Khlebnikov; ill. N. Burlyuk,
K. Malevich, P. Filonov. (SPb.:)
EUY, (1914). 48p., (16) leaves
of plates. 21 x 15cm. 1,000 copies.
(Kn.1.no.7696. 13-20 March)

"ВЛАДИМИР МАЯКОВСКИЙ": трагедия
("Vladimir Mayakovsky": a tragedy)
V. Mayakovsky; ill. V. & D. Burlyuk.
M.: ("Lit. Ko" Futuristov "Gileya"),
1914. 44p., (7) leaves of plates.
17.7 x 13.5cm. 1,000 copies.
(Kn.1.no.8655. 27 March-3 April)

ФУТУРИСТЫ: ПЕРВЫЙ ЖУРНАЛ РУССКИХ
ФУТУРИСТОВ (Futurists: First Journal
of the Russian Futurists). no.1-2.
ed. V. Kamensky; ill. D. & V. Burlyuk,
A. Ekster. M., 1914. 157p., (4) leaves
of plates. 28.3 x 20.3cm.
(Not in Kn.1. Publ. before 22 March)

ТАНГО С КОРОВАМИ: железнобетонные поэмы *
(Tango with Cows: ferroconcrete poems)
V. Kamensky; ill. V. & D. Burlyuk. M.:
(Izd. Pervogo Zhurnala Russkikh
Futuristov), 1914. 19.7 x 19.7cm. 300
copies.
(Kn.1.no.8856. 27 March-3 April)

ВОЙНА: мистические образы войны
(War: mystical images of war)
N. Goncharova. M.: V.N. Kashin, 1914.
Portfolio of 14 lithographs. 36.5 x
27cm.
(Not in Kn.1.)

СТРЕЛЕЦ. Сборник первый (The Archer.
no.1) ed. A. Belenson. Пг., 1915.
216p., (12) leaves of plates. ill.
25.5 x 18.5cm. 5,000 copies.
(Kn.1.no.7091. 4-11 March)

ПРОПОВЕНЬ О ПРОРОСЛИ МИРОВОЙ
(A Sermon-Chant about Universal
Sprouting)
P. Filonov. (Pg.:) Mirovyi raztsvet,
(1915). 24p. ill. 23.2 x 18.3cm. 300
copies.
(Kn.1.no.8482. 11-31 March)

ВЕСЕННЕЕ КОНТРАГЕНТСТВО МУЗ
(The Vernal Forwarding-Agency of the
Muses) ed. D. Burlyuk, S. Vermel';
ill. V. & D. Burlyuk, A. Lentulov.
Spring 1915. M: Studiya D. Burlyuka
i Sam. Vermel', 1915. 107p. 27 x 20cm.
500 copies.
(Kn.1.no.12545. 19-26 May)

ЗАУМНАЯ ГНИГА (Transrational Book)*
A. Kruchenykh, Alyagrov; ill. O.
Rozanova. M., 1915. 21.9 x 19.4cm.
140 copies.
(Kn.1.no.19058. 11-18 Aug.)

ТАЙНЫЕ ПОРОКИ АКАДЕМИКОВ
(Secret Vices of the Academicians)
A. Kruchenykh, I. Klyun, K. Malevich.
(M., 1915.) Cover date: 1916. 32p.,
(1) leaf of plates. ill. 22.8 x 18.3cm.
450 copies.
(Kn.1.no.19059. 11-18 Aug.)

ВЗЯЛ: барабан футуристов
(Took: a Futurists' Drum)
V. Mayakovsky (et al.); ill. D. Burlyuk.
Pg., 1915. 15p. 34.7 x 24.5cm. 640
copies.
(Kn.1.no.25316. 16-31 Dec.)

ВСЕЛЕННАЯ ВОЙНА (Universal War)*
A. Kruchenykh. Pg., 1916. 22 x 33
cm. 100 copies.
(Kn.1.no.3903. 25 Feb.-3 March)

ЧЕТЫРЕ ПТИЦЫ (Four Birds)
D. Burlyuk, G. Zolotukhin, V.
Kamensky, V. Khlebnikov; ill.
A. Lentulov, G. Zolotukhin. M.:
Izd-vo K., 1916. 96p. 23.1 x 18.7
cm. 480 copies.
(Kn.1.no.4660. 3-10 March)

МОСКОВСКИЕ МАСТЕРА: журнал искусств
(Moscow Masters: arts journal)
V. Khlebnikov (et al.); ill. A.
Lentulov (et al.) M., 1916. 100p.,
(10) leaves of plates. 26.6 x 19.8
cm. 1,000 copies.
(Kn.1.no.7517. 26 April-3 May)

СОЛНЦЕ НА ИЗЛЕТЕ (The Spent Sun)
K. Bol'shakov; (cover) ill. El.
Lisitsky. M.: Tsentrifuga, 1916.
63p. 23.4 x 18.8cm. 480 copies.
(Kn.1.no.10466. 28 June-5 July)

ОТ КУБИЗМА И ФУТУРИЗМА К СУПРЕМАТИЗМУ:
Новый живописный реализм (From
Cubism and Futurism to Suprematism:
new painterly realism)
K. Malevich. 3rd ed. M., 1916. 31p.,
(2) leaves of plates. ill. 18 x 13cm.
5,000 copies.
(Kn.1.no.16408. 7-14 Nov.)

НЕУВАЖИТЕЛЬНЫЕ ОСНОВАНИЯ
(Weak Foundations)
I. Aksenov; ill. A. Ekster. M.:
Tsentrifuga, 1916. 46p., (2) leaves
of plates. 35 x 26.5cm. 200 copies.
(Kn.1.no.758. 12-19 Jan. 1917)

УЧИТЕСЬ ХУДОГИ (Learn Art)
A. Kruchenykh; ill. K. Zdanevich.
Tiflis, 1917. (26) leaves. 23.5 x
19cm.

В.В. КАНДИНСКИЙ (V.V. Kandinsky)
    text & ill. V. Kandinsky. M.:
    Otdel Izobrazitel'nykh Iskusstv
    Narodnogo Komissariata po Prosveshcheniyu
    1918. 56p., 30.2 x 21cm.

О НОВЫХ СИСТЕМАХ В ИСКУССТВЕ
    (On New Systems in Art)
    text & ill. K. Malevich; cover
    El. Lisitsky. Vitebsk: Artel'
    khudozhestvennogo truda pri
    Vitsvomase, 1919. 32p., (3)
    leaves of plates. 22.3 x 19cm.

ЗАУМНИКИ (Transrationals)
    A. Kruchenykh, G. Petnikov,
    V. Khlebnikov; ill. A. Rodchenko.
    (Pg.:) EUY, 1922. 24p., (1) leaf
    of plates. 21.3 x 14.5cm.

ЛИДАНТЮ ФАРАМ (Le-Dantyu as a Beacon)
    Il'yazd. Paris: 41°, 1923. 61p.
    19.1 x 13.3cm.

82. *Hermits*, 1913:
back cover showing list of books
published by Kuzmin
and Dolinsky; lithograph.

SELECT BIBLIOGRAPHY

ANDERSEN, TROELS *Malevich-Catalogue raisonné of the Berlin Exhibition 1927* . . . Amsterdam, Stedelijk Museum, 1970

BANN, S. & BOWLT J. E., eds. *Russian Formalism. 20th-century studies.* Edinburgh, Scottish Academic Press, 1973

BAROOSHIAN, VAHAN D. *Russian Cubo-futurism 1910–30.* The Hague/Paris, Mouton, 1974

BOWLT, JOHN E., ed. *Russian Art of the Avant-garde: Theory & Criticism 1902–34. The Documents of 20th-century Art.* N.Y., Viking Press, 1976

BURLIUK, DAVID, ed. *Color and Rhyme,* (Hampton Bays, N.Y.), 1930–66

CHAMOT, MARY *Gontcharova.* Paris, La Bibliothèque des Arts, 1972

CHAMOT, MARY 'Russian Avant-garde graphics' *Apollo,* (London), December, 1973

COHEN, ARTHUR A. 'Futurism & Constructivism: Russian & Other.' *The Print Collector's Newsletter* (N.Y.) Vol. VII No. 1, March–April, 1976

COMPTON, SUSAN P. 'Malevich and "the fourth dimension".' *Studio International* (London) Vol. 187 No. 965, April, 1974

COMPTON, SUSAN P. 'Malevich's Suprematism – The Higher Intuition' *The Burlington Magazine,* Vol. CXVIII No. 881, August, 1976

GRAY, CAMILLA *The Great Experiment in Russian Art 1863–1922.* London, Thames & Hudson, 1962

GEORGE, WALDEMAR *Larionov.* Paris, La Bibliothèque des Arts, 1966

GIBIAN, G. & TJALSMA, H. W., eds. *Russian Modernism – Culture & the Avant-garde 1900–30.* Ithaca & London, Cornell U. Press, 1976

HARRISON, GAIL *Constructivism & Futurism: Russian & Other.* Ex Libris 6. N.Y., J. Art Inc. 1977

KAMENSKY, V. *Ego-moya biografiya velikogo futurista.* Moscow, 'Kitovras', 1918

KARSHAN, DONALD *Malevich, The Graphic Work: 1913–30.* Jerusalem, The Israel Museum, 1975

KHARDZHIEV, N. 'Mayakovsky i zhivopis.' *Mayakovsky: materialy i issledovaniya.* Moscow, Nauka, 1940

KHARDZHIEV, N. & TRENIN, V. *Poeticheskaya kul'tura Mayakovskogo.* Moscow, 1970

KHARDZHIEV, N. 'Pamyati N. Goncharovoi i M. Larionova' *Iskusstvo knigi,* (Moscow), 1968

KHARDZHIEV, N., MALEVICH, K. & MATYUSHIN, M. *K istorii russkogo avangarda / The Russian Avant-garde.* Stockholm, Hylaea Prints, 1976

KOVTUN, E. F. 'Varvarara Stepanova's Anti-Book.' *From Surface to Space, Russia 1916–24.* Exhibition catalogue, Galerie Gmurzynska, Cologne, 1974

KOVTUN, E. F. 'K. S. Malevich. Pisma k M. V. Matyushinu.' *Ezhegodnik rukopisnogo otdela Pushkinskogo doma na 1974 god.* Moscow, Nauka, 1976

KOVTUN, E. F. *Knizhnye oblozhki russkikh khudozhnikov nachala XX veka.* Katalog vystavki, Gosudarstvennyi Russkii Muzei, Leningrad, 1977

KRUCHENYKH, A. *15 let russkogo futurizma, 1912–1927.* Moscow, 1928

LIVSHITS, B. *Polutoraglazyi strelets.* Leningrad, 1933

LIVSHITS, B. *The One and a Half-Eyed Archer.* Trans. John E. Bowlt, Newtonville, Mass., Oriental Research Partners, 1977

LOGUINE, TATIANA *Gontcharova et Larionov, cinquante ans à Saint Germain–des-Prés.* Paris, Klincksieck, 1971

MALEVICH, K. S. *Essays on art 1915–33.* Vols. I-III. Ed. Troels Andersen, trans. X. Glowacki-Prus & A. McMillin. London, Rapp & Whiting/André Deutsch 1969–7

MALEVICH, K. S. *The Artist, Infinity and Suprematism. Unpublished Writings 1913–33.* Vol. IV. Ed. Troels Andersen, trans. X. Hoffman. Borgen, Copenhagen, 1978

MALEVIC[H], K. S. *Scritti,* Ed. A. B. Nakov, Milan, Feltrinelli, 1977

MARCADÉ, V. & J.-C., *'La Victoire sur le Soleil' – Edition bilinge. Théâtre Années Vingt.* Lausanne, L'Age d'Homme, 1976

MARCADÉ, V. *Le Renouveau de l'Art Picturale Russe 1863–1914.* Lausanne, L'Age d'Homme, 1971

MARKOV, V. 'The Longer Poems of V. Khlebnikov.' *Modern Philology* Vol. LXII. U. of California Press, 1962

MARKOV, V., ed. *Manifesty i programmy russkikh futuristov. Slavishche Propylaen, Band 27.* Munich, Fink, 1967

MARKOV, V. *Russian Futurism – A History*. London, Macgibbon & Kee, 1969

MARKOV, V., ed. *A. E. Kruchenykh: Izbrannoe/Selected works*. Munich, Fink, 1973

MICHELIS, C. DE *Il futurismo Italiano in Russia 1909–29, temi i problemi*. Bari, De Donato, 1973

NAKOV, A. B. *Malevitch Écrits*. Paris, Champ Libre, 1975

NAKOV, A. B. 'Malevich as Printmaker.' *The Print Collector's Newsletter*, (N.Y.), Vol. VII No. 1., March-April, 1976

POMORSKA KRYSTYNA *Russian Formalist Theory & its Poetic Ambience*. The Hague/Paris, Mouton, 1968

SHKLOVSKY, V. *Mayakovsky and his Circle*. Trans. & ed. Lily Feiler, London, Pluto Press, 1974

INDEX OF ILLUSTRATIONS

Numbers refer to pages on which black and white illustrations are shown;
colour plate numbers are given in bold figures.

INDEX

Russian titles in the index are given in English translation
omitting the definite or indefinite article (which is not
expressed in the original) e.g. *Word as such (Slovo kak takovoe)*.